Hind:

2023

A collection of 11 short plays marking the third annual international festival at Left Edge Theatre.

Originally produced by Left Edge Theatre in front of a live audience on July 23, 2023.

Contact the playwrights directly for permission to produce their play.

Table of Contents

Act 1

Act 2

Act I

Adeline

By Allison Moon

About the playwright:

Allison Moon is the author of five books including the instant classic sex-ed guide Girl Sex 101. Inspired by her sex education work, Moon writes screenplays, stage plays, and teleplays that explore the complexities of identity, sexuality and eroticism, particularly when interfacing with technology. She has a degree in Neuroscience and Theatre from Oberlin College and an MFA in Creative Writing for the Performing Arts from UC Riverside.

Her play ZERO STATE was an O'Neill Semifinalist (2022) and part of the Bay St. Theater's 2022 Title Wave New Works Festival. THE TIP OF THE TONGUE was produced in the 2021 Fresh Fruit Festival of LGBT Plays and received a reading at the Come Inside Theater Festival in Portland, OR. She received two special recognitions from the Kennedy Center American College Theater Festival for writing and directing an adaptation of LYSISTRATA. Read her work at alliedmoon.com

---

ADELINE was directed by Skylar Evans.

TRAVIS   Sam Minnifield
ADELINE   Allie Nordby

CHARACTERS

TRAVIS: 28, Black man
ADELINE: 26, White woman

<u>Setting:</u> Oakland, California. Night.

_____

Two adjacent backyards, separated by a wooden privacy fence. The house on the left is weathered but homey. It has a motion sensor light over the door. The house on the right is a new gut job, gentrification special. This backyard has a hot tub.

Travis steps through the metal security door, triggering the motion sensor light. He lights a joint and sits on the top step. After a moment, the light goes out.

The door on the right opens and Adeline steps onto the deck, wearing a spa robe and sandals. She drops her robe and relaxes inside the hot tub.

Travis stays still, trying not to look but easily seeing from his perch.

After a few moments, Travis extinguishes the joint and moves to reenter the house. As he reaches for the door the motion sensor light bursts on.

Adeline shrieks and covers herself.

TRAVIS

I didn't see anything! I didn't see anything I swear.

Adeline laughs nervously.

TRAVIS
Sorry, I didn't mean to scare you.

ADELINE
Don't worry about it. I didn't realize—

TRAVIS
Sorry—

ADELINE
That's your house, you have nothing to apologize for.

TRAVIS
Yeah no. From this angle, I definitely can't see anything.

ADELINE
Okay.

TRAVIS
It's not, though.

ADELINE
Not what?

TRAVIS
My house. I'm visiting my moms. Bunch of people in there.
Just needed a break.

ADELINE
Oh right. Happy Thanksgiving.

TRAVIS
Yeah. You too.

ADELINE
I'm just visiting for the weekend. Do you know Dan and Zahir?

TRAVIS
Just waves over the fence. You doing Thanksgiving with them?

ADELINE
They're in China.

TRAVIS
Oh, word.

ADELINE
Zahid has some academic conference. I'm their surrogate.
Which is why I'm housesitting.

TRAVIS
They're not brothers?

ADELINE
Dan and Zahid?

TRAVIS
Yeah.

ADELINE
Zahid is from Yemen. Dan is from Buffalo. They're married.

TRAVIS
I don't need to know all that.

ADELINE
But your moms...

TRAVIS
What about her?

ADELINE
Your parents are lesbians.

TRAVIS
What?!

ADELINE
You said you're visiting your moms.

TRAVIS
Oh oho oh. Yeah no, yeah, no. It's like a / slang—

ADELINE
/ Black—

TRAVIS
Sure, yeah. Lesbian parents. Shit.

Long awkward pause.

ADELINE
You having a tough family moment or something? Sorry, that's
nosy. Mothers are diff—

TRAVIS
She's actually my mother-in-law, but I call her mom.

ADELINE
Oh, that's unique.

TRAVIS
It is?

ADELINE
Maybe not. Not my thing, but cool. I was always jealous of the
kids who had, like, those open door policies in their house.
Friends and family coming and going all the time. Or I don't
know, maybe it sucks.

TRAVIS

Nah, it's pretty good. Always someone to look after you, do you a favor, or just, like, tell you how to live your life.

ADELINE

Eesh.

TRAVIS

It's family.

ADELINE

How long have you been married?

TRAVIS

I'm not.

ADELINE

But you have a—-

TRAVIS

We were never married. We just called each other wifey and hubby. Young and dumb cute shit, you know? She lives in Houston now. Got a new man.

ADELINE

Oh, sorry.

TRAVIS

It's all good. We were high school sweethearts.

ADELINE

That never works out.

TRAVIS

A few of my friends are still with theirs.

ADELINE

Good for them then.

TRAVIS
What are you doing for Thanksgiving?

ADELINE
I don't celebrate it.

TRAVIS
You one of those, what are they, Jehovah's Witness?

ADELINE
I dated a Native guy in college. He took me to Alcatraz for
Thanksgiving, or what they called Day of Mourning. I can't
really stomach the holiday now.

TRAVIS
My mom makes the best mac and cheese ever. I'm never
letting that go. Plus I get my kid every other year.

ADELINE
You have a kid?

TRAVIS
Marshall. Turned eleven last month. You wanna see a picture?

ADELINE
Uh...

TRAVIS
Right. Later.

ADELINE
You must've been...

TRAVIS
Like I said. Young and dumb.

ADELINE
Is that hard?

TRAVIS

Seeing another man raise my son isn't great. But he's a good guy. It's better for them down there. More room. They come up most summers because those Texas summers, phew.

ADELINE

Yeah, the Bay Area is superior in terms of climate.

TRAVIS

For now.

ADELINE

Yeah.

TRAVIS

I'm Travis, by the way.

ADELINE

Adeline...

TRAVIS

Like the street.

ADELINE

What?

TRAVIS

Adeline. A big street, right over there.

ADELINE

Oh.

TRAVIS

You didn't know that?

ADELINE

I'm not from around here.

TRAVIS
It's like two blocks away.

ADELINE
I took an Uber.

TRAVIS
Where are you from?

ADELINE
...

TRAVIS
Or not, whatever.

ADELINE
Boise.

TRAVIS
Cool.

ADELINE
You've been?

TRAVIS
Nah.

ADELINE
You're not missing anything.

TRAVIS
So why you in town with these mans' baby without them
here?

ADELINE
I have some doctor's appointments.

TRAVIS
And they don't wanna be here?

ADELINE
It's early yet. Eight weeks.

TRAVIS
Doc's gonna see you over the holiday?

ADELINE
I guess so.

TRAVIS
Not to get into your business, but you probably shouldn't be in
a hot tub.

ADELINE
Oh. It's-— I'm fine probably.

TRAVIS
It's just that your body can think you have a fever and--
y'know.

ADELINE
I'm probably fine.

TRAVIS
Just not good for the baby is all I'm saying.

ADELINE
What about what's good for me?

TRAVIS
What's good for the baby is what's good for you.

ADELINE
Is that so?

TRAVIS
Yeah it is so. Everything you do is for that little one now.

ADELINE
It's not my baby. It's Dan and Zahir's.

TRAVIS
They'll be the kid's dads or whatever, but you'll always be its mom.

ADELINE
I don't think I believe that.

TRAVIS
Believe it. You wanted it. You're doing it. It's yours. Gotta own that.

ADELINE
Oh, I gotta "own it"?

TRAVIS
Mmhm.

ADELINE
[...] Want to join me?

TRAVIS
Oh, no, yeah, I'm good. No, yeah, no.

ADELINE
I didn't / mean.

TRAVIS
Yeah no it's / cool.

ADELINE
Like I meant I was going to go put on a swimsuit—

TRAVIS
I got family inside I should get back to.

ADELINE
Before you--— I lied. My name is Em.

TRAVIS
Okay...?

ADELINE
I don't know. You're a stranger. I guess I thought I needed to
protect myself.

TRAVIS
Alright... I lied, too. I did see
something. Not much. But. Something.

He moves to exit.

ADELINE
Hey, could I have a hit of that?

TRAVIS
Uh...

ADELINE
Here, let me—-

*She exits the hot tub. Travis turns away. She puts on the robe
and reaches over the fence.*

TRAVIS
Listen, I don't want to, like, mansplain pregnancy but...

ADELINE
I'm not pregnant. Not yet.

TRAVIS
Oh.

ADELINE
Sorry.

TRAVIS
For what?

ADELINE
Lying.

TRAVIS
You can lie to a stranger.

ADELINE
Well you're kind of my neighbor so that feels worse.

TRAVIS
Only temporary.

ADELINE
Well for now you're my neighbor. And I feel bad lying.

He hands her the joint. She takes a drag.

TRAVIS
You wanna see a picture of Marshall now?

ADELINE
Who?

TRAVIS
My kid.

She shrugs. He shows her his phone over the fence.

TRAVIS
I took him to Legoland in August.

She's stopped looking.

TRAVIS
Anyway he's a good kid. Really into building stuff. I think he's
going to be an engineer.

She passes the joint back over the fence.

TRAVIS
Alright. Well. Be seeing you.

ADELINE
Hey Travis, wait. I lied.

TRAVIS
You do that a lot huh?

ADELINE
I guess so.

TRAVIS
You don't have to come clean with me about everything. I'm
never going to see you again. Or well I guess if you'll be
coming around more I will.

ADELINE
Would you like that?

TRAVIS
What?

ADELINE
To see me around more?

TRAVIS
You seem cool.

ADELINE
You sure about that?

TRAVIS
You not sure about that?

ADELINE
I'm here for an abortion.

TRAVIS
...Alright.

ADELINE
I guess I don't have to lie about it here. But Idaho and the laws
it just... felt better to be quiet about it.

TRAVIS
So you are pregnant.

ADELINE
Yeah.

TRAVIS
How far?

ADELINE
Eight weeks. That was true. Sorry if you think I'm trash.

TRAVIS
I don't--! Damn. You're not trash. I just feel bad is all.

ADELINE
For me?

TRAVIS
And the baby. And the daddy.

ADELINE
Don't.

TRAVIS
I mean, I do but alright.

ADELINE
Don't.

TRAVIS
Can I feel bad for you then?

ADELINE
...No.

TRAVIS
Alright... When's your appointment?

ADELINE
Tomorrow. Seven a.m.

TRAVIS
How are you getting there?

ADELINE
Uber I guess. Or maybe I could do one of those e-scooters I'm
seeing all over. They look fun.

TRAVIS
Might be hard to ride back after, though.

ADELINE
Right. Yeah.

Long pause.

TRAVIS
I could drive you.

ADELINE
What?

TRAVIS
I got a car. It's not luxury or anything, but I can drive you.

ADELINE
Really?

TRAVIS
I'm an early riser.

ADELINE
Okay. Travis? Thank you.

TRAVIS
No worries. I got you, mama.

END OF PLAY

Celebrities in Space

Jessica Moss

About the playwright:

Jessica writes, performs, and produces. Some of her plays include Funnie (2022 winner of the Leah Ryan's FEWW Prize, O'Neill finalist), Our Play (2023 winner of the Lanford Wilson award), A Girl Lives Alone (SafeWord New Play Contest winner), Cam Baby (Toronto Fringe New Play Winner, Weissberger finalist), Polly Polly (Ed Mirvish Award for Entrepreneurship), Next to Him, We'll Make it Together, and more. Her TYA show, The Worries of Wesley, will premiere in January at the Contemporary Theatre of Ohio, and Our Play, an ensemble piece for high-school and university students, will premiere at Southeast Missouri State University in February. Training: Juilliard.

CELEBRITIES IN SPACE was directed by Zane Walters.

BLAKE	Ryan Severt
OLENDOWSKI	Caitlin Strom-Martin
CALLAGHAN	Mike Pavone

CHARACTERS

BLAKE: A NASA spacey type person guy, any gender
OLENDOWSKI: A NASA spacey type person guy, any gender
CALLAGHAN: A NASA spacey type person guy, any gender,
likely a bit older than Blake or Olendowski, old guard, big
George C. Scott or Ed Harris energy (not that they have to be
male, that is, but those are the references that I have at the
moment, you know?).

Setting: Offices at NASA. Bleep bloop blorp.

*A '/' marks point of interruption where the following line
begins.*

A frustrated office.
Probably machines that go BING!, if you have them? Or also
nothing. Nothing works great.
CALLAGHAN and BLAKE pace, or sit, exhausted, frustrated, and
completely out of ideas.
BLAKE opens their mouth as if they had an idea.
CALLAGHAN eagerly looks to BLAKE.
BLAKE pauses…. Closes their mouth. Shakes their head.
CALLAGHAN pounds their fist.

CALLAGHAN
Goddammit. Are we ever going to come up with an idea?
Well, Blake, /are we?

BLAKE
I don't know, boss.

CALLAGHAN
You don't know. Goddammit. Well we better figure it out,
Blake.

BLAKE
I know, boss.

CALLAGHAN

Or it's curtains for us. Imagine. All these years I been at NASA. All these years, as a spacey type person guy, exploring the final frontier. Pushing science to the limits so that we could better understand our place in the universe. And now, declining interest. Declining funds. With earth going to shit, they say, "maybe we should spend the money here, on making lives better, more liveable on earth, instead of looking around in space". And if we don't come up with something that'll make space travel seem relevant, exciting, worthwhile...goddammit.

BLAKE

We'll be out to sea.

CALLAGHAN

Out to sea? We'll be out to space. Goddammit.

OLENDOWSKI bursts in.

OLENDOWSKI

I've got it. I've really got it.

BLAKE

No.

OLENDOWSKI

I do. I can hardly believe it, but -

CALLAGHAN

Don't toy with me, Olendowski, I can't take it.

OLENDOWSKI

I really think I've got it. Celebrities. In space.

Beat.

BLAKE
My God —

CALLAGHAN
What the hell did you just say?

OLENDOWSKI
I said Celebrities. In space. We take celebrities. We send them
to space.

Beat.

BLAKE
Boss, I think Olendowski's got it.

CALLAGHAN
It couldn't work.

BLAKE
Why not?

OLENDOWSKI
I know it sounds crazy. But these are crazy times, aren't they?
In days like these you gotta think outside the box, you gotta
shoot for the stars, but that's what we do, goddammit. We're
NASA and we shoot for the stars.

BLAKE
Boss, we're dreamers.

CALLAGHAN
I know we're dreamers, goddammit, but we're also spacey
type person guys, goddammit. We need to know our
limitations. We have to be rational, goddammit, we've got to
be practical.

BLAKE
Hear Olendowski out, at least, boss.

CALLAGHAN (...)
All right, Olendowski, I'll hear you out, what's the idea?

OLENDOWSKI
It's celebrities. In space.

CALLAGHAN (...)
My god.

BLAKE
What more do you need other than that? That's incredible, it tells you the whole thing.

CALLAGHAN
It's catchy, I'll give you that.

BLAKE
It sure could boost the profile of the space program. NASA sure could use something that got people's attention like that, boss. Could change everything for us, could be the answer we're looking for. Celebrities. Wow.

OLENDOWSKI
In space.

BLAKE
Wow.

CALLAGHAN
You can't let yourself get sucked in by flashy ideas, flashy ideas fizzle out, I just need to understand this, make sure I'm seeing all angles of the proposition. Walk me through it.

OLENDOWSKI
I gotcha, boss. So, we take celebrities, right?

CALLAGHAN
What kinda celebrities?

OLENDOWSKI
All kinds. Whatever kinds you like. Actors, rock stars, football
players, billionaires

BLAKE
Oprah?

OLENDOWSKI
We couldn't get /Oprah.

CALLAGHAN
We'd NEVER get Oprah, goddammit.

BLAKE
Goddammit.

OLENDOWSKI
But there's bunches of 'em, and they all have a following. So
we take those celebrities....

BLAKE
Yeah? Yeah?

OLENDOWSKI
And we send 'em to space.

BLAKE
Wow.

CALLAGHAN
All right, all right. Don't get your hopes up. You got something
there, Olendowski, you got something, but I got a lot of
questions. First off, where in space do we send 'em?

OLENDOWSKI
Just.... Space.

OLENDOWSKI *makes sound effect like: "out there"*

CALLAGHAN
All right, all right. Do we train 'em?

OLENDOWSKI (...)
Kinda.

CALLAGHAN
Kinda.

OLENDOWSKI
Yeah, like we train 'em, but we don't train 'em.

CALLAGHAN
All right, all right.

BLAKE
This is genius! You've really done it, Olendowski!

CALLAGHAN
Now goddammit, Blake, don't go getting excited. It solves our problem, sure, but it's so crazy, how could it work?

BLAKE
Or... it's so crazy it just might work?

CALLAGHAN
Goddammit, Blake. You just blew this wide open. All right, all right, how do we get the celebrities to do this?

OLENDOWSKI
Here's the thing, Boss: they want to do it. They're signing up left, right, and center. They all want a piece of the pie. And here's the thing, Boss: we can charge 'em

BLAKE
Wow!

CALLAGHAN
Charge 'em?

OLENDOWSKI
Millions of dollars for the privilege.

BLAKE
My god, we could fund new explorations.

OLENDOWSKI
New explorations, improved technology, state-of-the-art
innovations

BLAKE
New chairs in the computer /room?

OLENDOWSKI
And new chairs in the computer room.

CALLAGHAN
GODDAMMIT, I don't want us getting excited about new
chairs in the computer room, we've all had our hearts broken
too much.

BLAKE
Ah, but, boss, you gotta see that this is a sure thing. This really
could make it all happen for us. The attention, the money, I
could meet Oprah.

CALLAGHAN
OPRAH ISN'T GONNA /DO IT.

OLENDOWSKI
Oprah isn't gonna /do it.

BLAKE
She might! We're talking about a world where the richest
more privileged people get to hop in a rocket and go into

space, with no education or business being there. Anything is possible!

CALLAGHAN
My goddammit.

OLENDOWSKI
Whaddaya think, boss?

CALLAGHAN (...)
In my many years here at NASA in the Spacity-Space program, I never saw times as hard as these. I never thought that the farther we'd be able to travel, the more we'd have to go. The more we learned, the more we'd have to learn. But you, Olendowski. You come in here with a plan that can save us all. Goddammit, kid. Goddammit.

OLENDOWSKI
You like it, boss?

CALLAGHAN
Like it? I love it. Celebrities into space. What an idea. What an achievement. The most beautiful and famous among us riding around in a little space suit. And when they come back, the stories they'll be able to tell, and the more we'll be able to grow our little program. You've really done it, Olendowski.

OLENDOWSKI (...)
Come back?

CALLAGHAN
Yeah, you know. When they come back from space.

OLENDOWSKI
Oh. Uh. Hm. I mean…. Uhhhh. Uh. Uhhhhh. Yeah, interesting.

CALLAGHAN
Well, surely we'd… we'd bring them back.

29

OLENDOWSKI
Uh huh. Uh huh. Uh huh. Definitely an idea there. Definitely a
possibility. Not really what I was thinking, but –

BLAKE
You were suggesting we just sorta…. Launch them out there?

OLENDOWSKI
Yeah, you know. *(OLENDOWSKI does a little mime of chucking
someone out into space)* Hwup. Off ya go. Enjoy!

CALLAGHAN
And then… just….

OLENDOWSKI
Yeah, I dunno, float? What really happens up there, anyway,
we ever been able to figure that out? They'll, you know, chill.
Post a selfie. And then ….

BLAKE
And then what?

OLENDOWSKI
Well I don't know, but…. *(OLENDOWSKI does a little mime like,
"they would disappear")*. What, I thought you guys were
onboard.

CALLAGHAN
I just assumed they would be coming back.

OLENDOWSKI
But why would we do that, what good would that do?

BLAKE
We're trying to bring awareness to space travel so that we can
keep going as a company!

OLENDOWSKI
And I told you, they'd pay! Tons of revenue coming in, plus, the press before? Pfft. It'd be great. Today Show, CNN, get people from the networks, I'm sure some of 'em would love it. It would definitely bring awareness. We're gonna launch Kanye into space? Who doesn't watch that?

BLAKE
Ye.

OLENDOSKI
Yay, exactly! It solves our problem. It solves most problems.

BLAKE
Who'd do this once they realize what was going on?

OLENDOWSKI
You can make literally anything popular these days! People are paying millions for NFTs! Y'know what those are?

BLAKE
I've heard of them but I don't understand them.
OLENDOWSKI
Exactly! That's what they are. Things you hear about but don't understand, and they are selling them for millions! And I mean, maybe we'd have to clump 'em together, make a day of it! Cause, yeah, I could see interest declining at a certain point, BUT STILL!

BLAKE
No, but... but you'd be killing people.

OLENDOWSKI (...)
We'd be killing celebrities. Not exactly the same thing.

BLAKE
Some of the most beloved people –

OLENDOWSKI
Who control the vast majority of wealth, continue to increase that incredible wealth by throwing balls or playing pretend, or getting to live out their wildest dreams and fulfill their creative potential while the rest of us play basketball on the weekends or do community theatre and work our bodies to complete collapse to be able to afford a completely sub-optimal existence? Look Blake. You work here every day. You've worked here every day for years. Do you get paid enough?

BLAKE
I —

OLENDOWSKI
You like in a studio apartment with a hotplate.

BLAKE
I'm saving for an Oculus.

OLENDOWSKI
Did you think you'd be down here, in the offices, with the fluorescent lights and the no windows? Didn't you think, when you devoted your life to astroscience, that that meant you'd spend your entire life on the ground floor? Didn't you want to be the one actually going to space? Didn't you want to soar, Blake? Didn't you want to soar?

BLAKE (...)
Yeah.

OLENDOWSKI
And if some idiot billionaire, who has done nothing but pollute the world that the rest of us are stuck on while it turns and burns, who has created something that makes your life a living hell, that is designed to make you hate yourself, but is also designed to be so addictive and foundational to our interactions that you literally can't leave even though you develop this small pain in your lower stomach that never goes

32

away because of it, if that billionaire, with his billions decides that he should be lucky enough to participate in the miracle of space travel, for NO reason other than his ill-gotten wealth, how does that make you feel.

BLAKE (...)
Bad....

OLENDOWSKI
And so should we let that billionaire return to the planet that he was largely responsible for destroying?

BLAKE (...)
No.

OLENDOWSKI
No. No we should not, Blake.

BLAKE
Screw him.

OLENDOWSKI
Exactly. Exactly, Blake, screw him.

BLAKE
Launch him up there. Launch 'em all up there.

OLENDOWSKI
And you see, it's self-selecting. The only celebrities who are going to think that this program is for them, is something they're worthy of, are the most selfish, self-aggrandizing, worst people on earth.

BLAKE
BUT NOT FOR LONG!

OLENDOWSKI
EXACTLY! Exactly!

CALLAGHAN
Goddammit!

OLENDOWSKI (...)
Boss?

CALLAGHAN
Goddammit, Olendowski... you're a genius.

OLENDOWSKI
Really, boss?

CALLAGHAN
You think you've done all you can. You think there must be a
limit at some point. To the universe, sure. To the limits of
space travel. But also to human ingenuity: to how much we
can come up with, how much we can do. And then, and idea
like this comes in. To launch famous people into space and
leave 'em up there. And it's humbling, really. It makes you feel
big, and oh so small. It makes you shocked at how much we're
capable of, and makes you wonder who else we can throw
into the void for a few extra dollars? It's remarkable. It makes
me proud to be a spacey type person guy. You did it,
Olendowski.

OLENDOWSKI
No. We did it.

*They all shake hands. They shake hands again. They slap each
other's backs. CALLAGHAN picks up a phone, and dials.*

CALLAGHAN
Houston? We have a solution. *(beat)* Oh, I'm sorry, hit 9 first
to dial out?

END OF PLAY

34

Liberal State

Michael P. Adams

About the playwright:

Michael P. Adams is an award-winning writer from the greater Los Angeles area. His plays have been produced in New York (Atlantic Theater Company), Los Angeles, Albuquerque (Fusion Theatre Company), Memphis, Spokane, and Tucson, among others. Michael is also a member of the Playground-LA writers' pool.

_____

LIBERAL STATE was directed by Jenny Hollingworth.

DANI   Sam Minnifield
MELISSA   Lexus Fletcher

CHARACTERS

DANI: Genderfluid, but currently presenting as female; late 20's-early 30's
MELISSA: Female, mid 30's

Setting: *A neighborhood playground. Morning. The present.*

AT RISE: DANI sits on a bench, a nervous energy about her. While genderfluid, she presents here as a very recognizable version of a female: a mother in need of a break. She watches her (offstage) child play.

DANI
(to the child) No, Parker, I don't want to push you on the swing right now. Mommy just needs a minute to –

She gives up the thought, not worth the effort.

MELISSA, bright-eyed and Lululemoned, takes a seat on the bench. She calls out to her (also offstage) child.

MELISSA
Good job, sweetie. Yes, you're such a strong little climber.
(to Dani)
Hello.

DANI
Hi. She really is a good climber. Fast.

MELISSA
I haven't seen you here before.

DANI
We just moved here. From Lubbock. We moved from Lubbock, Texas, to Portland. You already know we're in Portland. Obviously you know that. I'm sorry. I talk too much sometimes. I use more words than I should, which is the same

36

thing as saying I talk too much, which I just said. I'm gonna stop talking now.

MELISSA
I'm Melissa. Don't worry. I don't bite.

DANI
A name. See, that's such an easy way to keep from blabbing the way I do. Say your name and let that be the end of it. Not that I mean we have to stop talking because you said your name and that's the end of it. Sorry, new people... God... My name's Dani.

MELISSA
On the plus side, I found out everything I needed to know about you and I didn't even have to ask a single question.

DANI
That's everything?

MELISSA
I was kidding.

DANI
Yeah, no. I know that. I totally got that.

MELISSA
Which one's yours?

DANI
Hm? Oh, uh, red jacket, big head.

MELISSA
She's cute. And her head looks perfectly normal to me.

DANI
They.

MELISSA
I'm sorry?

DANI
Not she. They.

MELISSA
(slightly condescending) Really.

DANI
(nervousness fading) Yes, really.

MELISSA
How old is she?

DANI
(stronger) They.

MELISSA
Right. How old is... they? *(doesn't sound right)* Is they? Are they?

DANI
Are. Still are. And they are three years old.

MELISSA
You're letting her -- I keep doing that -- letting them choose? I'm not even sure I know how that's possible. *(to her child)* Wow, you went down that scary slide. You're so brave.

DANI
(re: the slide or the topic at hand?) It's not that big a deal. *(quick beat)*They are whoever they want to be.

MELISSA
Forgive me for being a little crass –

38

DANI
You are welcome to be crass. I may not forgive you for it.
(off Melissa's confusion) Go ahead.

MELISSA
Oh, well, um, they have genitals, I assume. Of course they
have genitals. Everyone has genitals. Ha. Looks like you
transferred some of your nervousness over to me, ha ha. But
seriously...

DANI
I want you to imagine someone -- a complete stranger --
coming up to you, maybe you're with your husband at a nice
restaurant on your anniversary or you're looking for a new
purse at the mall -- and that person starts asking you
questions about your genitalia. Would you respond favorably
to that?

MELISSA
I most certainly would not.

DANI
Then why the fuck do you think it's okay to ask me questions
like that about my kid?

MELISSA
It's a natural curiosity, I think. Maybe you have one of those
hermaphrodite children.

DANI
And if I did, then the question would be appropriate?

MELISSA
This is why I prefaced it with --

DANI
What about your kid?

MELISSA
My...?

DANI
Your little angel.

MELISSA
I don't think we need to get snippy with each other.

DANI
She has a vagina?

MELISSA
Yes.

DANI
Describe it for me so I know for sure.

MELISSA
I won't do that.

DANI
Oh, come on. I'm very interested in the details of your child's
vagina. *(no response from Melissa)* I can wait.

MELISSA
You've made your point. *(a beat)* Can I ask why, though?

DANI
Why what?

MELISSA
Why don't you just let them be a boy or a girl?

DANI
Because there's no such thing.

MELISSA
As a woman, I beg to differ.

DANI
What does that mean, "as a woman"?

MELISSA
Well, since you don't want to talk about genitalia anymore,
I'm not going to answer that.

DANI
So that's the only thing that defines you? Your body?

MELISSA
I'm pretty proud that I can still rock a little black dress.
Besides, without our bodies, we'd be nothing but walking
skeletons.

DANI
Which is funny, 'cause we all have the same bones. Let me ask
you this: Am I a woman? In your eyes? Do I check off all the
boxes?

MELISSA
Of course. You're a mom.

DANI
Today.

MELISSA
I don't understand.
DANI
That is the most sensible thing you've said so far.

MELISSA
But I really don't.

DANI
Tomorrow when I wake up, I might feel like being a dad. And I might want to put this hair up in a man bun. And wear boxers under cargo shorts.

MELISSA
So you're trans? I have no problem with trans people.

DANI
No.

MELISSA
A crossdresser?

DANI
People always want to make it about the clothes.

MELISSA
You're the one that mentioned boxers.

DANI
Not trans. Not a crossdresser. Non-binary. Genderqueer. Genderfluid. Whatever you want to call it.

MELISSA
And if I don't want to call it anything?

DANI
That's a choice, too, I guess. You're confused, I can see that.

MELISSA
Is this, like, a split personality?

DANI
It is simply being free enough to express all of me.

MELISSA
Did you give birth to your child?

DANI
And we're back to genitalia.

MELISSA
I'm sorry. I'm not trying to be obtuse, I just –

DANI
You can let yourself off the hook. You aren't the first person
that doesn't know what to do with me or my parenting
decisions. It's okay. I thought this place was supposed to be
crazy liberal, though. I'm a little disappointed so far.

MELISSA
That's why you moved here?

DANI
One of several reasons. My ex decided he'd been tolerating
me long enough. Liked me plenty when I was in girl mode,
liked to rough me up in boy mode.

MELISSA
So you did give birth.

DANI
That's the takeaway from that story, huh? ... He started to get
rough with Parker, too, calling them names, and that's when I
knew I had to get out of there. He gave me one last punch in
the stomach and told me he hoped he never saw either of us
again.

MELISSA
I'm glad you got away from him... You're raising Parker to be
like you.

DANI
I'm raising Parker to realize for themself who they want to be.

MELISSA
But children don't get to choose that. No one gets to choose that.

DANI
Exactly. I know you didn't intend to support my argument right then, but you actually did. It's not a choice. We either have our gender foisted upon as at birth or we find out later on that we were living the wrong life and start living the right one. Either way, not a choice. Just being who we're supposed to be.

MELISSA
You're going to make life very difficult for them.

DANI
Life's hard for everyone. It's even harder when you don't allow yourself to be authentic.

MELISSA
Easy for you to say. You're an adult. Are you going to be able to sell that line when Parker comes home with a black eye?

DANI
If you and the rest of the moms at this park do your jobs right, I shouldn't have to worry about Parker coming home with anything other than a smile.

MELISSA
That's what it really comes down to. You all just want to be catered to.
DANI
If being treated with kindness and respect is the same thing as being catered to, then yes, cater away.

MELISSA
You're oversimplifying.

DANI
Am I?

MELISSA
Yes, this issue goes way beyond… No, I see what you're doing.
You're trying to goad me into saying something else that you
can twist to fit your agenda.

DANI
Am I?

MELISSA
I'm not taking the bait.
(to her child) Sweetie, it's time to go… No, we'll come back
another time, when the park's not so crowded… Now!

DANI
Afraid I'm going to indoctrinate you?

MELISSA
No, we have an appointment to get to.

DANI
Uh-huh. Has anyone ever called you Mel?

MELISSA
Of course. My friends call me Mel all the time.

DANI
That's a boy's name.

MELISSA
It's a nickname.

DANI
Maybe. Is there a possibility that when they call you Mel,
maybe you're doing something that society considers more
masculine? Like maybe you're drinking a brewski and

watching the game and all of a sudden it's a chorus of "Who'd you pick to win, Mel?" and "Can you believe that pass, Mel?" But when it comes to asking you which QB is the hottest, I'll bet they call you Melissa again. Or maybe you're out on the range shooting your firearm and the power of that steel in your hand just makes you feel more like a Mel.

MELISSA
I'm a Portland parent. I don't have a gun.

DANI
You see what I'm getting at, though. When your daughter does something that you think only boys should do -- play in the dirt or look for insects -- do you encourage it?

MELISSA
She doesn't like doing those things.

DANI
All kids like doing those things. If they're allowed to do them.

MELISSA
That's a little different than telling your child that they can pretend to be a boy one day and a girl the next.

DANI
Nobody's pretending. It's instinctual. It's completely natural.

MELISSA
You and I have different definitions of natural.

Melissa stands, picks up her bag.

DANI
We'll be here tomorrow. Parker and I.

MELISSA
And...?

DANI

I don't know. Maybe you will be, too? You'll see how happy this little person is that they get to express themself however they want to. You'll see it in me, too. If you wanted to get to know me.

MELISSA
And if I don't?

DANI
Now that is a choice.

MELISSA
It was nice -- Goodbye.

DANI
(as Melissa starts to walk away) Hey, Mel.

Melissa turns, looks a little pissed off, dare we even say... masculine?

MELISSA
What?

DANI
(satisfied)
Nothing. Never mind.

END OF PLAY

Adult in the Room

By Greg Vovos

About the playwright:

GREG VOVOS is a playwright, screenwriter, theater director, and Senior Writer at American Greetings. He's a two-time winner of the Ohio Arts Council Individual Excellence Award in Playwriting; a Cleveland Public Theatre Nord Playwriting Fellow; Dobama Theatre Playwrights Gym member; and Dramatists Guild member. Greg was resident playwright for the Willoughby Fine Arts Association's Theatre for Healthy Living Program for whom he's written 15 plays about issues facing youth today. His work has been seen around the world, translated into several languages, and published by several outlets. He's taught playwriting at various theatres and universities, including University of Nevada, Las Vegas, Baldwin Wallace University, and Case Western Reserve University, where he teaches today. He earned his MFA in Playwriting from UNLV and a B.A. in English from The Ohio State University. He's married to his best friend and together they have two amazing kids and a lot of pets.

───────────────────────

ADULT IN THE ROOM was directed by Seth Dahlgren.

GODFREY   Mario Herrera
KELSEY: Julianne Bradbury

CHARACTERS

GODFREY: A high-school aged boy who is tired of watching.
KELSEY: Godfrey's hardworking mom who's doing her best to take care of her kids in a world that makes that very difficult.

Setting: *The family's kitchen. Weekday morning.*

At rise: The family kitchen. GODFREY gets ready for the school day. He puts on his headphones, throws on his jacket, and stuffs a gun into his backpack. His mom, KELSEY, enters and spies what he's doing.

KELSEY
Godfrey?

He can't hear her through his headphones. Kelsey pulls at his arm.

KELSEY
Godfrey!

Godfrey takes off his headphones.

KELSEY
What are you doing?

GODFREY
Going to school. Why?

KELSEY
Do you have a gun?

GODFREY
What? No.

KELSEY
I saw you put what looked like a gun into your backpack.

49

GODFREY
I don't know what you're talking about.

KELSEY
Let me see your backpack.

GODFREY
I'm late.

Godfrey tries to push past her but she grabs his backpack. They struggle for it, but Godfrey wins. Kelsey falls to the ground.

GODFREY
Oh, jeez, Mom, why...are you okay?

She stands.

KELSEY
I'm fine.

GODFREY
Good. I'm sorry.

Godfrey heads out.

KELSEY
You're not leaving here until you tell me what's in your bag.

GODFREY
Nothing.

KELSEY
Either you show me now or I'm calling the police.

GODFREY
You're going to call the cops on me? On your son?

KELSEY
If my son is taking a gun to school, then yes.

GODFREY
I'm not.

KELSEY
Then show me.

Pause. No movement by either. She pulls out her phone. Dials. It RINGS. Someone picks up and Kelsey holds out her phone so Godfrey can hear.

VOICE ON PHONE
Water Falls PD.

Godfrey takes the gun out of his backpack and shows her. She hangs up the phone.

3

KELSEY
Jesus, Godfrey.

GODFREY
You happy now?

KELSEY
Where'd you get that?

GODFREY
Uh, it's not exactly against the law, so...

KELSEY
What do you plan on doing with it?

GODFREY
Nothing.

KELSEY
Give me the gun, Godfrey.

GODFREY
Mom, you don't understand what you're doing.

KELSEY
Give me the gun.

She reaches for it and he aims it at her. She freezes. Long silence.

KELSEY
What are you doing?

Godfrey lowers the gun. Puts it back in the backpack.

GODFREY
It's not what you think.

KELSEY
You don't know what I'm thinking.

GODFREY
You think I'm going to shoot up my school.

KELSEY
No, I'm thinking my baby boy has a gun and I have no idea why. I'm thinking I must not know a damn thing about your life because this is not the son I raised. I'm thinking I just want you to put it down before someone gets hurt.

GODFREY
Someone is going to get hurt.

KELSEY
Godfrey, please. What are you planning to do?

GODFREY
Don't worry about it.

KELSEY
Oh, thank you for that advice. Yes, I'll just stop worrying about it. Problem solved.

GODFREY
Look, there's this kid in my history class. And I know for fact that he's planning on shooting up the school. So I'm going to get him before he gets the rest of us.

KELSEY
What? How could you know this?

GODFREY
Uh, because I've lived my entire life in a world where kids shoot up their schools. Because school shootings are all over my timeline. Because I spend every moment of every school day with some part of my brain on alert watching and studying each kid to see if they have the characteristics of a mass shooter. And because I've identified one. And now, I'm going to eliminate him.

KELSEY
Eliminate him? Jesus, Godfrey.

GODFREY
It's okay, Mom. Trust me. I'm not wrong on this.

Godfrey pulls a journal out of his backpack.

GODFREY
This is his journal. I copped it from him two days ago.

Godfrey hands her the journal and points to a specific section. Kelsey reads the section. Her eyes widen as she does. It's horrifying.

KELSEY
My God...

GODFREY
See? It's happening. Today. I don't have time. I have to go.

KELSEY
We have to get this to the school, to the police.

She dials her phone. He rips the phone out of her hands.

GODFREY
Are you fucking kidding me? They won't do anything. This kid brought weapons into school two weeks ago and yet he's still going there. They don't do shit. And the cops don't care.

KELSEY
Of course they care. They just—

GODFREY
They don't do shit. So I'm going to.

KELSEY
You don't know what you're talking about.

GODFREY
I know exactly what I'm talking about. See, while everyone's been tweeting and doing whatever bullshit it is they do, like sending thoughts and prayers, I've been preparing. Because the cops, the administrators, the quote "ADULTS IN THE ROOM"...you people don't do shit. Because the criminals who run this country are all beholden to the NRA and the gun manufacturers. Meanwhile, the money-grubbing capitalistic bullshit society we live in is squeezing the living soul out of every one of us kids. So excuse me when I don't put any fucking trust whatsoever into them. Because I don't. And even those that really do care, like you, are honestly too scared to do anything about it. Because even though you watch in

54

horror on TV, there's a part of you that still doesn't believe it can happen in our school. But it can and it is. And you don't know how to stop it, because you don't live through it. Not really. But I do. And I will. *(He takes the journal back and sticks it in his backpack.)* I don't want to see any of my friends or classmates BUT ONE die today. And when the news interviews me, and asks why I did this, I'll tell them. I'll tell them because adults couldn't solve the problem, so we are. And then if I see any motherfucking gun-toting assholes praise any of this, I'll shoot them too.

KELSEY
My God.

GODFREY
Yeah.

KELSEY
Then you're just proving them right. A good guy with a gun theory, is that it?

GODFREY
What do you propose?

KELSEY
We take a breath. We tell the police.

GODFREY
Again with the cops? Did you not see Uvalde?

KELSEY
That was just one—

GODFREY
No. Nope. Sorry.

KELSEY
You'll get killed, Godfrey. You're just a kid and you'll—

GODFREY

I'm just a kid. That's right. And that's fine. I don't want to be an adult. I don't want to fail the world the way adults have. All things being equal, I'd rather die a kid than become one of you. I'm sorry.

He starts to leave. She gently grabs him by the hand and he stops.

KELSEY

I know this might seem like a good idea to you right now. And I know the adults have completely failed your generation. But this isn't it. You trying to be the hero, isn't it. Because even if you do shoot him, then what? You have to live with that for the rest of your life? That you killed someone?

GODFREY

That I killed a killer? Sure, why not?

KELSEY

And what if he doesn't go through with his plan and you shoot him and end up in jail yourself?

GODFREY

He's going to—

KELSEY

Or in the process you kill or injure someone else?

GODFREY

I'm not going to hurt anyone else.

KELSEY

You don't know that.

GODFREY

I do.

KELSEY
How can you know that?

Pause as he takes her in.

GODFREY
You don't believe in me.

KELSEY
Oh, Christ. Yes, I believe in you, which is why I can't let you
leave here!

GODFREY
Except you can't stop me.

He pulls away from her.

KELSEY
You're right. I can't. But we can alert the school. You can text
your friends. Snapchat it, TikTok, whatever you guys use.
There's another way.

GODFREY
That won't stop it. Maybe that helps this one time, but it
won't put an end to—

KELSEY
I know it feels like risking your life and future is the answer
because you don't want to become an adult. But we need you
to become one. I do. The world does.

Pause.

GODFREY
Mom, I love you. I mean that. And I don't want to cause you
any pain so believe me when I tell you I'm going to be as
careful as I can. But I can't sit by like this anymore, feeling
powerless, hoping for the best. No more. People need to know

they can't get away with this shit. And I know you care. But this...this world I live in...you don't understand it like I do. (*He gives her back her phone.*) Here. Take your phone back. And you do what you need to do. I respect that. But I gotta do what I gotta do. And I hope you respect that.

Godfrey gives his mom a big hug and a kiss on the cheek. He leaves.
Mom stares after him, then out at us.
Then...she dials her phone. It RINGS.
She hangs up.
She looks out at us...Deep breath.
She again dials her phone. It RINGS and RINGS...
Blackout.

END OF PLAY

The Donor Class

By Scott Carter Cooper

About the playwright:

Scott Carter Cooper's work is tailored to small professional companies with diverse ensembles looking for economical plays to produce. His short-form pieces have been successful with Chicago companies including American Blues, The Artistic Home, Chicago Dramatists, and a number of smaller storefront companies. Internationally, his plays have been produced in Canada, Ireland, England, Germany, India, China and Hong Kong. Cooper holds a BFA – Theatre from Drake University and an MA – Writing from DePaul University.

THE DONOR CLASS was directed by David L. Yen.

HE	Mark Bradbury
SHE	Julianne Bradbury
DOC	Anthony Martinez

CHARACTERS

HE: Male, 30's
SHE: Female, 30's
DOC: Male or Female, any age

Setting: *A clinical waiting room. A sign for the clinic with a benign tagline at the back. A couple in their late 30's or early 40's enter. They seem to know what they're doing as they take a seat.*

SHE
Did you remember to take the peanuts out of Rebecca's lunch bag?

HE
Yes.

SHE
The school is serious about nuts. She'll be sent home if she has any in her lunch bag.

HE
I know. There are no nuts.

SHE
I don't want her embarrassed in front of her class.

HE
I took care of it.

There's a pause.

SHE
Did Jordy look a little pale to you?

HE
He's fine.

60

SHE
Are you –

HE
I'm sure. Relax. We've talked this through a hundred times.

SHE
I know.

HE
You said this is the best thing for the family. And you're
helping someone else.

SHE
I know.

HE
This was all your idea, but we don't have to do this if you
don't want to. It's not your responsibility to –

SHE
I know. But—

HE
We'll find the money somewhere, else. If we have to.

SHE
No. I read all the literature you brought home. This is what
makes sense. I mean, we're done having kids, right?

HE
We can't afford any more.

SHE
I know. And if I don't do this now –

HE
I know.

SHE
I'm not getting any younger.

HE
No.

SHE
The time is now. They won't want me in a few years.

HE
Look. Look at me. We have a beautiful family. We'll find the money someplace else if you don't want to do this.

SHE
Where?

There's a pause.

HE
I don't know. But we will.

SHE
Oh God.

HE
I love you.

An androgynous person enters, carrying a clipboard and wearing a lab coat. Severe looking, but not unkind.

DOC
You must be 769-AJ-7. Yes?

HE
Yes.

DOC
I apologize for the informality of numbers, but we've found anonymity makes things easier for the contributor and recipient. And you're here to –

SHE
Make a donation. Yes, that's right.

DOC
Well, of course you understand that strictly speaking you're not making a donation. This is an outright sale. You will be liable for any tax implications.

HE
Yes.

DOC
We find things are easier if we refer to this part of the process as a contribution.

HE
We understand.

DOC
Because that's what you're doing; contributing to another family and helping them have children they might not otherwise have. Financially speaking you have the option to receive payments over time, which will result in a higher payout, or to receive a lump sum, which will result in a lower price and most likely a higher tax penalty.

HE
Yes. We understand. We've decided on the lump sum. Isn't that right, honey?

SHE
Yes.

DOC
Very good. As described in section 907-C of the contract, if you go that route, based on your age and if the medical examination verifies your statements, we are prepared to issue a check today for three hundred thousand dollars.

HE
Wow.

SHE
That's a lot of money.

HE
Yes.

SHE
Will it be enough? Two kids.

HE
I would think so. And then some. We could get you the deluxe vacuum, and maybe a dishwasher too.

DOC
Many of our contributors come here specifically to fund college tuition for their children. Is that your goal? Of course, what you do with the money is your business.

SHE
Of course, that's our main reason. College. Yes.

HE
Yes.

DOC
While we can't guarantee tuition costs when your children are of college age, we do have some discount agreements with some of the major universities in the country.

SHE
Which ones?

DOC
I'm not at liberty to say at this time. A full list can be made available once you've signed the confidentiality agreement, your contribution has been made and payment accepted.

SHE
I see.

DOC
But I guarantee, you'll be pleased.

SHE
Oh. That's nice.

DOC
So, if everything is in working order. Let's begin. Have there been any injuries or illnesses that might impact fertility?

SHE
No.

DOC
Excellent. Now, the price we've determined is based on age and verification of functionality, so if you'd please come with me, we'll put you through some basic testing.

SHE begins to follow the DOC.

DOC
No ma'am. We'll just need your husband for the next couple of hours. Once we've harvested the unit, and it's been accepted, you can come back to collect him. It should be about two hours.

SHE

No. I'm the one. You're harvesting my unit.

DOC

I don't understand.

SHE

I already have two children. I don't need my ovaries or uterus any longer, so I'm the one making the contribution.

HE

We think it's the right time to share her reproductive unit with a family who's been less fortunate.

DOC

Oh. I see.

SHE

Is there a problem? They don't want me. You don't want me?

DOC

We're just not accepting female contributions at this time. There is not a strong demand for female units. I thought this would have been explained to you. We harvest male units. Everyone wants a working penis these days. Sometimes it's a question of aesthetics. Sometimes it's an issue of functionality. There are various reasons. We're on a schedule here, but quickly. This is quite a competitive market. The base price of three-hundred thousand dollars covers the harvesting of the prostate and testicles, leaving you with a penis. There are prosthetics and hydraulics we can provide to render the remaining equipment somewhat functional, but nothing works like the original. In certain situations, primarily where there is a particularly pleasing complete unit, we can make an additional offer for the penis, depending on history of performance and aesthetics. In which case ma'am, you would be required to complete and affidavit swearing to the ability of the penis to sexually satisfy the female partner.

SHE
Oh.

HE
That's not what we –

SHE
And how exactly is the bonus determined?

HE
WHAT?!?

SHE
They don't want women, honey. You heard the doctor.
Everyone wants a penis now. Women aren't wanted, are they
doctor.

DOC
I'm not sure I'd say that exactly, but historically speaking I
think we can all agree, the contributions of women have been
severely under-valued. So, applying the logic of the free
market, we've simply found a way to monetize the most
prized aspect of man. His organ. Again, I think we can all agree
that the way we value the male organ has shaped much of
human history.

SHE
Honey?

HE
What?

SHE
What do you think?

HE
You want me to be castrated?

SHE

You heard the doctor. Your penis is the most valuable thing we have. Of course, that all depends on how the bonus is calculated.

DOC

We pay by the inch.

SHE

Oh. Still, honey, you said every little bit helps.

HE

But we came here for you.

SHE

No. We came her for the children. You said we can't afford any more children, so we should share our good fortune with those who've been less fortunate.

HE

But we agreed you'd be making the contribution.

SHE

But didn't you say we needed to do whatever we could for our children? Isn't that why we're here? Money? For the children?

HE

Wait.

DOC

I understand your apprehension. But I assure you it's perfectly safe. We extract the sex organ from the contributor and replace it with an extendable plastic tube system that allows for fluid waste and sexual stimulation for your female partner.

SHE

See?

HE
But –

DOC
The tube comes in an assortment of sizes and colors.

SHE
Ooh. Did you hear that honey? Colors! Such as?

DOC
And prints!

SHE
Do you have a Burberry?

DOC
It's coming out next fall.

SHE
Oh.

DOC
But, something to look forward to with our bi-annual flush and
fresh maintenance plan.

HE
Why are we even talking about this? I'm not doing it.

SHE
But they come in colors.

HE
But –

SHE
How much do you pay per inch?

DOC
One hundred thousand for the first four inches, and then one
million dollars for each additional inch.

SHE
Think of that! Think what we can do with an additional
hundred thousand dollars.

HE
But –

DOCTOR
Perhaps I should give you a few minutes to discuss. But don't
take too long.

The DOCTOR exits.

HE
You realize what this means?

SHE
It's for the children, honey.

HE
That's when we were talking about –

SHE
About me?

HE
We can still have a normal life if you don't have a uterus or
ovaries. Things are very different if I don't have a penis.

SHE
Is that right?

HE
YES!

SHE

Well, I'm going to go out here and look at color chips and I'll
let you stay here and think about what I was prepared to do
for our family, and what exactly you're prepared to do. But
make your decision snappy, because we're on a schedule. And
remember. Colors!

*SHE exits as the lights slowly dim and close in on HE, who is left
standing in the waiting room, holding the brochure.*

END OF PLAY

Act II

Hope

By Dana Schwartz

About the playwright:

DANA SCHWARTZ is a Los Angeles writer, director, producer and actress. She is a member of the 2023 cohort at Director's Lab West. Her short play "The Crush" is currently running at the Echo Theater. "Presto!" was completed while working with The Workshop Theater in New York and is currently a 2023 O'Neill Semi-Finalist. "@Playaz" was a 2019 Eugene O'Neill Finalist and had its World Premiere in 2021. "Early Birds" premiered in 2019, and was also presented at the Curtis Theater. She has written for several productions of the internationally renowned Car Plays, notably at REDcat LA, Disney Hall, Segerstrom Arts and La Jolla Playhouse. She has directed plays across the country, and performed around the world. She produces the MADlab New Play Development Program at Moving Arts Theatre, where she is also a company member. Her plays can be found at https://newplayexchange.org/users/19341/dana-schwartz and www.danawritesplays.com

———————————————————

HOPE was directed by Cheryl King.

MALORY   Caitlin Strom-Martin
ANGEL   Mark Anthony

CHARACTERS

MALORY: 30's-40's, any race, dressed like she found her clothes somewhere. Several somewheres.
ANGEL: 40's-50's, Latino, a certain grace belies the fact that he also found his clothes somewhere

Setting: A crappy tent on a sidewalk in a hip neighborhood.

Inside a crappy tent. There is a large pile of blankets on one side of the tent. Outside, we see MALORY approaching. She walks by the tent, kicks it and quickly walks away. No response from inside, so she walks by again. Kicks it. Nothing. Giggling to herself, she wiggles inside. She sighs, stretches out, and notices the pile of blankets.

MALORY
Ooh!
She examines the top blanket, checks it for softness, smells the corner, makes a face. Then she shrugs and pulls the top blanket off the pile and covers herself with it. From under the remaining pile we hear a voice.

ANGEL
Occupied.

MALORY
AAAH!

We see the pile is actually ANGEL.

ANGEL
Shh!

She starts smacking him, he tries to stop her.

MALORY
What the hell man?

74

ANGEL
Quiet down! You want someone to come?

MALORY
Shit!

ANGEL
Watch your language.

MALORY
Are you fucking kidding me?

ANGEL
What?

MALORY
I'm a crazy old homeless lady, why should I have to watch my
language?

ANGEL
Well, I'm a crazy old homeless man and yet I still believe it's
important to conduct oneself with a modicum of propriety.

MALORY
You smell like pee and you're sleeping on a sidewalk.

ANGEL
Even so.

*Malory looks at him suspiciously. She sighs and starts to go.
She really doesn't want to though.*

MALORY
Fine. Whatever. What do you want?

ANGEL
Want?

MALORY
Yeah, what do you want. For me to sleep here.

ANGEL
What do you have?

MALORY
Ugh, fine, you want me to-

ANGEL
No no no. No. Please don't even say it.

MALORY
Oh what, I'm not good enough to –

ANGEL
Please! Stop. Stop it. I'm simply asking if there's anything you
might offer in exchange for sharing this very comfortable, if
not roomy, tent. For the night. Not sex. Something...useful.

MALORY
Sex isn't useful?

ANGEL
Not today.

MALORY
I have beef jerky.

ANGEL
And alas, I'm a vegan.

MALORY
Are you messing with me?

ANGEL
Beef jerky is perfect. Thank you. It's a deal.

Angel extends his hand to shake hers. Malory touches one finger, gingerly, and then pulls out a bag of jerky and hands it to him. Angel take a piece and examines it like Gordon Ramsay inspecting a filet mignion. The jerky meets his approval, and he delicately takes a bite, chewing thoughtfully, a beautiful smile lighting up his face.

ANGEL
Exquisite.

MALORY
It's fucking jerky.

ANGEL
Please?

MALORY
It's jerky.

ANGEL
It's perfect. Have some.

She takes a big piece and shoves it into her mouth.

MALORY
(with her mouth full) Thanks. It's getting cold at night again-

ANGEL
Would you mind terribly, just, finishing your snack before telling this story?

Malory glares at him, chewing exaggeratedly and swallowing.

MALORY
Good jerky.

ANGEL
Angel.

MALORY
Oh, I'm agnostic.

ANGEL
My name. It's Angel.

MALORY
A little on the nose, don't you think?

ANGEL
Sometimes.

MALORY
I'm Malory.

ANGEL
Unfortunate. Ill fated.

MALORY
Fuck you.

ANGEL
That's what your name means. It's French.

MALORY
Yeah. I know. Fuck you.

ANGEL
An odd choice.

MALORY
You should meet my mother.

ANGEL
Do you ever wonder? What they thought when they named
you?

MALORY
I'm pretty sure she was thinking, "Where's my martini?"

ANGEL
I see.

MALORY
What about your mom Angel?

ANGEL
Her motive seems obvious, does it not.

MALORY
I guess. She around?

ANGEL
No. For a long time now.

MALORY
Lucky.

ANGEL
Excuse me?

MALORY
You didn't disappoint her.

ANGEL
Her life was a series of pleasures as well as regrets. But she
died before I was... So for that, yes, I am grateful.

MALORY
Cool.

ANGEL
Where are the rest of your things?

MALORY
None of your fuck-

ANGEL
Please?

MALORY
None of your FUCKING business.

ANGEL
I see.

MALORY
Look, let's not do this. I'll sleep here tonight, move on
tomorrow. Just eat the jerky and get some sleep.

ANGEL
Wise. Why bother.

MALORY
Exactly.

They sit in silence for a moment, eating.

MALORY (cont'd)
I had a spot at the park. But the cops roused everyone last
night and I've noticed there've been no lights on up here for a
while, so I figured I'd take a peek and see if I'd get lucky.

ANGEL
It's serendipity.

MALORY
If you say so.

ANGEL
Do you know what-

MALORY

Look dude, you can complain about my cussing, my manners, you can even turn down sex, but I'd really appreciate it if you don't assume I'm an idiot.

ANGEL

You're right. I apologize. It's only that I know prolonged drug use can do funny things to the-

MALORY

So now I'm a crack whore.

ANGEL

I was going to say meth.

MALORY

Gin.

ANGEL

I see.

MALORY

I don't do drugs.

ANGEL

Smart.

MALORY

Maybe I should. Who fucking cares now right?

ANGEL

There's a pot dispensary right around the corner.

MALORY

I don't think CBD gummies are going to help me at this point.

ANGEL

Might be fun.

MALORY
A blow job might be fun but apparently that's off the table.

ANGEL
I'm gay.

MALORY
No shit?

ANGEL
A gay, vegan, Hispanic painter.

MALORY
You should be the Mayor, not crashing in some gentrified
alley.

ANGEL
Indeed.

MALORY
It sure can turn on a dime, can't it.

ANGEL
You're telling me. I've lived in this neighborhood since the
1970's. Before you were born probably.

MALORY
Probably.

ANGEL
I watched it go from gang infested, drive-by nightmare to
liberal paradise in less than a decade. My mama paid nothing
for that house. I sold it some flipper for $500, thought I
robbed her blind!

MALORY
She sold it for twice that I bet.

ANGEL
Exactly.

MALORY
So what happened? You pissed away $500k? That seems
pretty stupid. Drugs?

ANGEL
Pride. Greed. Rent. Maybe a few drugs.

MALORY
Tried to play the system huh?

ANGEL
Tried and failed.

MALORY
Funny. I bought mine for 5.

ANGEL
Oh?

MALORY
Up on Garden Drive?

ANGEL
I know it well.

MALORY
Sweet little 2 and 1, figured I got in here in the nick of time.
The guy I bought from was so happy, it was like he won the
lottery. It was perfect. The Boulevard was getting hip. Safe.
Cute stores, good restaurants. Property values kept going up. I
had tenure. What could go wrong?

ANGEL
You were a teacher.

MALORY
8th grade biology.

ANGEL
Wow.

MALORY
I loved those crazy kids. Puberty is incredible. They were so weird and complex and interesting and constantly just, on the cusp of something. You know what I mean? I was great at it too. But the school board, and the charters... Even though I was there for almost 10 years I was the last one in. So.

ANGEL
I'm sorry.

MALORY
For some reason I can't seem to leave this neighborhood. Weird to panhandle the women who used to be in my hot yoga class.

ANGEL
Guys from the barber shop.

MALORY
Can't beat the hipster guilt though. I have about 50 of those stupid blessing bags.

ANGEL
How many toothbrushes do they think we need?

MALORY
Yeah. Man it is a short trip from a $6 pumpkin spice, to eating beef jerky in a tent with the only Vegan homeless guy East of Bronson.

ANGEL
Actually, there are quite a few of us. We meet on Sundays
after the Farmer's Market and gorge ourselves on Kale and
nostalgia.

MALORY
How very Ironic.

ANGEL
When in Rome.

MALORY
Right.

ANGEL
It's nice to be seen, you know? Past the labels. It's important.

MALORY
Fuck the labels, root of all evil in my opinion.

ANGEL
Perhaps.

Pause.

MALORY
What did you paint?

ANGEL
Murals mostly.

MALORY
No shit? Great murals around here.

ANGEL
I did the one on the corner off Fletcher, you know it?

MALORY
The one with all the Trees? I love that one. It got tagged
though.

ANGEL
Want to know a secret? It was meant to be tagged. It was a
statement. On the neighborhood. The layers. How these
complex, disparate visions come together and make
something new. Something even more beautiful.

MALORY
They painted over it last week. Now it's just gray.

ANGEL
A fitting end I suppose.

MALORY
I cried.

ANGEL
Thank you.

Pause.

MALORY
I'm so tired.

ANGEL
Why don't we stretch out a little, feet to head, body heat, get
some sleep?

MALORY
That sounds... yeah.

They shift around, get comfortable.

ANGEL
Maybe a new label? What's your middle name.

MALORY
Ha! I don't think that's gonna help either.

ANGEL
Tell me.

MALORY
(sighing) Hope. It's fucking Hope, can you believe that?

ANGEL
A little on the nose.

MALORY
You think?

ANGEL
I like it.

MALORY
Oh yeah? Maybe I'll try it out, see how it goes.

ANGEL
Good night Hope.

MALORY
Good night Angel.

They snuggle in.

END OF PLAY

Tom Cruise Saves the Planet

By Joni Ravenna

About the playwright:

Joni's plays include "A Brush With Fate" (West Coast Ensemble Theatre in Hollywood) and "For Pete's Sake" (DP Weekly Winner, Playwrights Circle Finalist, Nominated 'Best New Play' by OC Weekly following its long run at the Chance Theater in Anaheim), "The Green Grocer" (Dublin Fest Best Play, Finalist The Tulip Festival -NYC) and "Beethoven and Misfortune Cookies" which was produced at The Met, The Odyssey and the Wharton Center. A New Works of Merritt Honoree, it continues to be produced on the West Coast every year.

Ravenna is also co-author of "You Let Some GIRL Beat You? - The Ann Meyers Drysdale Story" which Forbes Magazine called, "A stunning portrayal of one of today's legendary women's basketball treasures."

Ravenna has written scores of articles for national and regional publications. Her new screenplay, "The Secret Notes of Professor Thomas," won the Plaza Classic Film Screenplay Competition 2022 and was selected by Impossible Dream Ent. (GET OUT, Black KKKlansman, Dayshift with Jamie Foxx).

———————————————————

TOM CRUISE SAVES THE PLANET was directed by Jenny Hollingworth.

TOM CRUISE	Mike Pavone
ELON MUSK	Mark Bradbury
JEFF BEZOS	Peter Downey
GRETA THUNBERG	Allie Nordby
VOICE	Zane Walters

CHARACTERS

TOM CRUISE - late 60's (still appears to be in his 40's) upbeat, ever smiling
ELON MUSK - late 50's , slight European accent
JEFF BEZOS - mid-late 60's, he is bald with a lazy eye
GRETA THUNBERG - In her late 20's, slight European accent
VOICE OF THE PILOT - Any age, gender, etc...

Setting: The year 2030. A high-speed interplanetary shuttle to Mars.

We hear the MISSION IMPOSSIBLE theme song. All characters are seated, leaning back stiffly, the heavy G-force plastering them to their seats. Simultaneously they sit up more naturally.

VOICE (OS)
Ladies and Gentleman having breached the earth's atmosphere, we can now safely increase velocity. ETA to Mars approximately three hours. Big round of applause to our Fearless Leader, Elon Musk.

ELON
(Bows to all, then to Jeff) Mr. Bezos, thank you for coming. I'm glad there are no hard feelings.

JEFF
Call me Jeff. And it's not who's first, Elon...It's who's best.

ELON
That's what I told Branson. He didn't listen. Now he's dead.

JEFF
Poor Richard. His shuttle exploding like that.

ELON
Instead of being first to colonize Mars, he was first to make New Mexico cough up bits of fuselage.

JEFF
And probably bits of him, poor bastard. Look Musk, I'm already turning down preorders. Hate to break it to you, but my baby will be the Rolls Royce to Mars. Make this tin can feel like a rickety ride at the fair.

VOICE (OS)
Folks if you peek through one of our starboard windows you'll see our beautiful blue Earth.

ELON
Care to peek through one of my starboard windows, Bezos?

VOICE (OS)
In the next hour you'll spot some of Earth's brothers and sisters. They'll appear yellow or grey. Saturn might look blue, but that's its rings fooling you. Neptune's methane is what makes it appear blue. You won't find any real blue out here. Earth is like a favorite child. Mother Nature and Father Time gave her everything they had.

We hear the VOICE belch over the speaker.

VOICE (OS) (CONT'D.)
Excuse me folks. That's never happened before. Apologies.

They all stare out in awe to the East, all but GRETA who stares at TOM CRUISE. TOM wears a baseball cap, incognito-like. GRETA scans the rest of the shuttle, shocked that Tom goes unnoticed by the twenty or so aboard. She stares back at Tom. Realizing he's been spotted, Tom lifts his index finger to his lips indicating she not blow his cover.

TOM
(approaches, smiling, whispering) I'm trying to scout a location for my next movie.

GRETA
(a little too loud) A movie about Mars starring Tom Cruise?

TOM
Shhh. Just one stunt, three tops. Hey, you're....

GRETA
Greta Thunberg.

TOM
I'm a big fan.

GRETA
(non-plussed) Thank you Tom Cruise.

TOM
(whispering) Call me Maverick. *(beat)* How is it you're here?

GRETA
-Yes, the expense was astonishing. But I've come to prove something vital *(retrieving a small, potted, plant from her purse, shielding it from the others' view).* With this Rhododendron I intend to demonstrate that Mars will never be habitable. The biosphere won't hold. Though I suppose when you and your crew die during the filming that will also prove my point.

TOM
They won't let you take that off the shuttle. No organic substances.

GRETA
(placing plant in purse) Once my suit is on and the oxygen and thermal apperati are secured, I'll sneak the plant into my suit. Once I place it on Mar's surface, and show it instantaneously evaporating into nothing, they'll all see. Mars is no place for us.

TOM
Wow.

GRETA
They'll understand it viscerally. The only way we understand
anything. On Instagram.

ELON
(to Jeff) Today, we'll be the first visitors to Mars. Soon, I will be
its most prominent landlord.

JEFF
It's got to be quadrillions of dollars to build a biosphere?

ELON
Our government's aware. Anything to save humanity.

JEFF
Listen, Musk, what do you say we pool our resources. Cut
Mark Cubin out of the Mars Race entirely.
Pretentioussonofabitch. *(He rubs a hand over his own bald
head.)*

ELON
(spotting Tom) Hey, isn't that...?

JEFF
(calling out, beating Elon to it) Tom! Over here.

Despite the order, it's Jeff and Elon who race to Tom.

ELON
(extending a hand to Tom, excited) I didn't see your name on
the Manifest. I would have comped you! *(realizing)* ... Oh, of
course..."Maverick!"

*Tom nods, then looks around, sheepish, hoping not to attract
even more attention.*

JEFF
Elon and I were just talking opportunities. We're like the early gold-miners without the beards and bad teeth.

ELON
(to Tom, attempting humor) Or in his case, without any kind of hair at all. And his eye? What's up with that? I keep wondering, is he flirting with me. *(laughs oddly)...* But all kidding aside, Tom, join us!

TOM
Look guys, it's never been about the money for me. I just want to make people smile.

ELON AND JEFF
Right.

JEFF
You singlehandedly saved Hollywood ten years ago with Top Gun, Maverick. We need you. Let's make a movie about how we're transforming Mars into a Shangri-La. With the Government's help of ...?

ELON
300 trillion. To start.

JEFF
Or what my ex-wife calls an amicable settlement.

ELON
You and Mackenzie split years ago.

JEFF
My latest ex-wife. Women! *(to Greta)* No offense.

TOM
I'm just scouting locations for a stunt, guys. Movie starts shooting next year.

ELON
On Mars? Too soon. You'll endanger the crew.

TOM
No, no. It's just me. *(beat)* I do all my own stunts. Do you know
when I shot Top Gun 1, I was the only guy not to faint under
all those G's.

JEFF
Tom, the biosphere's not ready. Even Elon knows that.

TOM
I can hold my breath for five minutes. It's just one stunt, four
tops. I've heli-skied down the Himalayas, motorcycled off
cliffs, jumped out of exploding buildings, swam through the
Amazon with crocodiles. Obviously we had to kill a few.

JEFF
You mean alligators...

TOM
My fans want more. They waited 34 years for Top Gun,
Maverick. I won't do that to them again.

ELON
No. Because in another 34 years you'll be like...a hundred and
five?

GRETA
(interrupting) Excuse me; but Tom, have you ever considered
that your career might be at least partly responsible for
polluting the earth? And therefore you're obliged to spend
your vast resources not on inane stunts, but on combatting
climate change.

ELON
Oh my God, here we go. "You celebrities with your jets and
mansions!" I brought back the EV after it was snuffed out by

94

the car industry in the twenties - perhaps the single greatest factor in reducing our carbon footprint- and even I get this shit, Tom. 'Elon built a Rocket because he has a small dick!' You can't win, Tom. Seriously. (*whispering*) Trust me, my dick's not small.

TOM

Maybe she's onto something. Risky Business definitely sold less tickets than every subsequent movie - except 'Eyes Wide Shut' ...Nicole's fault... You're right! My movies are partly responsible for the population explosion. They make people happy. Happy people have more sex.

ELON

That's not accurate.

JEFF

It's ridiculous. Rich people have more sex.

GRETA

Tom if you can save the movie industry, you can save our planet. Gentlemen, if you combine resources to save Earth we won't need Mars.

JEFF

Where's the profit in that?

GRETA

(*tearful, pulls plant out of purse*) On Earth, he breathes in what we breathe out. If we give him a little water and a little sunlight, he'll thrive. And if his brothers and sisters thrive, Earth thrives. We all thrive.

ELON

Greta, man is most happy when he's creating. (*catching himself*) Man and woman. But sometimes to create, you must first destroy. You consume, transform. There's waste. You're asking us not to create. But that's why we're here. To create.

95

Bigger, better, faster, stronger...To boldly go where no man - or woman - has gone before.

TOM

I don't create for the money or awards, Elon. I just want to make people smile. Really. But as a little boy, I'd climb on the roof, and look up at the stars and think, some day I'll visit my motherland.

The other three look at each other.

TOM (CONT'D)

We're all descendants of Extra Terrestrials. And one day, 23 And Me will confirm it. Greta aren't we allowed to reach for the stars?

JEFF

Or build big beautiful space crafts, or box-office smashes, or babies? ... We're put on this earth to create. What do you want to create, Greta?

GRETA

A solution! Growth is good, but cells that proliferate out of control are called cancers. If you terraform Mars the same solar winds that destroyed its atmosphere billions of years ago will destroy it again because Mars' magnetic field was also destroyed. Earth's field is ok.

TOM

Well, I guess maybe instead of terraforming Mars the plot could be about building a biosphere for Earth?

ELON

That would only increase the green house gasses. *(to Jeff, whispering)* He seems so smart in his movies.

GRETA

Tom, make a film where nothing gets blown up and everything gets made out of recycled goods. That will help. Do you know that because your country banned fluoro-carbons in aerosol cans 40 years ago, our ozone layer is healing! The UN Reported that the hole over Antarctica will be mended in approximately 35 years!

ELON

I'll still be ambulatory by then. Jeff, you're older. Tom's the oldest.

TOM

What if that's the plot?! I'm trying to save the ozone layer but Big Pharma is trying to destroy it, knowing they'll sell way more sunblock!

ELON

And Big Pharma is in league with Russia! If Russia's the bad guy I'll finance the movie!

TOM

(grabbing a pencil and paper) I like it.

GRETA

... And Mr. Musk, the Tesla is great. But you know they've found a way to generate more energy from fusion than the process requires. It's finally net positive. Fusion is cleaner.

JEFF

.... Tom, I want in on that movie too. Whatever Musk pledges, I'll double it.

GRETA

Mr. Bezos, maybe you could direct Amazon to connect people to regional centers where goods can be traded in person? Think of all the lonely people who'd benefit by engaging in human interaction to trade their wares. Less cardboard boxes shipped everywhere. And maybe the platform could facilitate business contacts, amateur athletics, even romance.

JEFF
(smiling) I'd put Match Dot Com and Tinder out of business in a week.

TOM
If we do this, will you do something for me, Greta?

GRETA
What?

TOM
Will you smile?

GRETA
If you do this Tom, there will be no reason not to smile. You'll have saved the planet.

VOICE (OS)
Uh oh, everybody better strap in...Boss, I'm not feeling so good. We hear alarm bells. And more belching.

ELON
Oh shit! There's no co-pilot. The aerodynamics required a small cockpit.

TOM
I can fly a rocket...For The Mars movie. Don't worry, guys. I got this!

The Mission Impossible theme song plays as Tom exits and the others smile in his direction adoringly. Lights out.

END OF PLAY

Molting

By Michael Towers

About the playwright:

Michael Towers is the Artistic Director of Westford Academy Theater Arts, the Summer School for the Performing Arts and Forge Theater Company. He earned his MFA in Playwriting from Boston University under the direction of Kate Snodgrass, Melinda Lopez and Ronan Noone. His short play, Pole Position, has been produced in Sydney, Australia and named a Short+Sweet Finalist in Hollywood, CA; Essex, UK; Perth, AU; Dubai, UAE, and most recently Illawarra AU. Pole Position was also awarded with The Honneger Prize for Best Short Play by the Firehouse Center for the Arts in Newburyport, MA. His new play, Molting has earned notoriety with stage, film and zoom productions in Boston, MA, Queens, NY, Cinnaminson, NJ and with the Village Playwrights' 10 Minute Play Contest during their June Pride Celebration. Molting earned the Judges Prize and the Audience Favorite Award in the 2023 Think Fast Short Play Festival sponsored by the Theater Project in Union, NJ. Most often, Michael's plays explore subjects that mystify and inspire him: the natural world, marriage, religion and the dynamic relationships between teachers and their students.

———————————————

MOLTING was directed by Skylar Evans.

DAUGHTER   Sylvia Whitbrook
FATHER   Ryan Severt

CHARACTERS

DAUGHTER: an 8-10 year old
FATHER: 30's to 40's

Setting: A table for two at a New England Seafood Shack

AT RISE: The DAUGHTER, appropriately bibbed, efforts the cracking of a lobster claw while her FATHER, sans bib, efforts to offer advice but keep a safe distance.

FATHER
Just

DAUGHTER
I'm trying

FATHER
Crack it

DAUGHTER
Crack...?

FATHER
Yes. Like...crack...

DAUGHTER
I'm trying

FATHER
It's more of a

DAUGHER
I can do it

FATHER
Crush

DAUGHTER
Crush?

FATHER
Do you need me to...?

DAUGHTER
I said I can

FATHER
Just

DAUGHTER
I can do it!

FATHER
Ok! Ok! Just

DAUGHTER
I don't want to hurt it.

FATHER
It's dead sweetheart. You're about to eat it.

*The DAUGHTER applies enough force: the lobster claw cracks.
She is struck in the face with fluid from lobster's shell.*

FATHER
Welcome to eating lobster.

*The FATHER hands the daughter a napkin which she uses to
wipe her face. A moment.*

DAUGHTER
Is this the sex talk?

FATHER
The what?

101

DAUGHTER
The sex talk.

FATHER
Why would you//say that...? No!

DAUGHTER
Is it?//Just tell me.

FATHER
Why would you think that?

DAUGHTER
I figured you were bribing me with something.

FATHER
Bribing you?

DAUGHTER
When you said we could eat "whatever I wanted wherever I
wanted."

FATHER
I don't...//bribe you

DAUGHTER
You do, dad. It's okay. But you do.

FATHER
Well

DAUGHTER
You've done it before

FATHER
I wasn't

DAUGHTER
So

FATHER
This time

DAUGHTER
I know when you're doing it.

FATHER
I mean:

DAUGHTER
And this feels like one of those times.

FATHER
Do you want to...?

DAUGHTER
Am I right?

FATHER
Have the sex talk?// Because:

DAUGHTER
No.

FATHER
We could if you wanted to.

DAUGHTER
I already had it.

FATHER
With...?

DAUGHTER
School. Duh. Who else?

FATHER
Of course. Duh. So...? What did they...say? About...?

DAUGHTER
If I tell you we'd be having the sex talk.

FATHER
I know. I know. But, were there...highlights?

DAUGHTER
If you mean projections//...yes. And they were big.

FATHER
Projections?? Of what?

DAUGHTER
I said: I don't want to talk about it!

FATHER
Got it. No sex talk.

DAUGHTER
Now what do I do?

FATHER
Oh. You...pull the meat out...

DAUGHTER
With my fingers?//That's kinda gross.

FATHER
There's a fork.//Inching closer to the moment of truth.

DAUGHTER
Now what?

FATHER
You eat it. Not that. That's the shell. Leave that. Yes. Now.
Deep breath. And just...

*The DAUGHTER places a small piece of the lobster meat on her
lips. She giggles as it falls out of her mouth repeatedly. They
both enjoy the silliness of the process.*

DAUGHTER
It keeps slipping!

FATHER
You need to

DAUGHTER
It's like rubber

FATHER
dip it

DAUGHTER
Dip it?

FATHER
in the butter. Yes.

DAUGHTER
How's that gonna help?

FATHER
Trust me.//It makes it

DAUGHTER
It's still gonna slip!

The DAUGHTER dips the small piece of lobster into the butter.

FATHER
More...familiar. I think. Easier to...

The DAUGHTER chews.

DAUGHTER
It tastes like rubber.

FATHER
How do you know what rubber tastes like?

DAUGHTER
It tastes like rubber dipped in butter.

FATHER
Everything tastes better in butter sweetheart. That's a
universal truth.

DAUGHTER
You're so weird.

FATHER
Was it everything you dreamed?

DAUGHTER
I didn't actually dream about it.

FATHER
Well, not necessarily dream

DAUGHTER
You always exaggerate.

FATHER
I don't always//...I was saying that because you were

DAUGHTER
Yes.//You always do.

106

FATHER
Excited

DAUGHTER
I wanted to try it. That's all. That doesn't mean I was dreaming
about it.

FATHER
Ok. Not like. Literally "dreaming." But. Excited. Right? Is that
an exaggeration? Can I say excited?

DAUGHTER
Yes.

FATHER
Great. You were excited. And now: What do you think?
Delicious?

DAUGHTER
I don't know. I guess I'll just have to...you know...wait and see.

FATHER
Well. I'm very proud of you for trying something new. New
can be scary.

DAUGHTER
I don't feel any different.

FATHER
You wouldn't have to feel different.

DAUGHTER
How will I know if it worked?

FATHER
Worked how?

DAUGHTER
If I'm immortal.

FATHER
Immortal?

DAUGHTER
Because lobsters are immortal.

FATHER
I don't think so...

DAUGHTER
They are, dad. They're "biologically immortal." My teacher
said.

FATHER
I really don't think that's true.

DAUGHTER
It is true. They don't actually die. Not from old age. Duh.
That's what it means. Only if they get a disease or have
problems with their shell molt...molting...or if they starve. Or if
people catch em. Or they get eaten. Which can be the same
thing but, if people do catch em and they have eggs, you have
to throw em back so they can make more lobsters but you
have to mark 'em first so no one else can take them either. "It
discourages the practice of eating females." If they're too
small, you have to throw them back too because they haven't
grown up yet and that wouldn't be fair and if they're too big,
you really have to throw them back because they've survived
this long already. It's one of the only animals in the kingdom
whose size is directly portionate to their age.

FATHER
Pro-portionate.

DAUGHTER
And those are the ones.

FATHER
The "ones"?

DAUGHTER
Who can live forever.

FATHER
Yeah?

DAUGHTER
Because they've made it this far. See? They're built to survive.

FATHER
And you thought: If you eat them...?

DAUGHTER
You are what you eat. You say it all the time.

FATHER
I do. Yes.

DAUGHTER
It's true, right? Or have you been lying?

FATHER
I haven't been//lying

DAUGHTER
Then it's true? Because if not, you'd be lying.

FATHER
Yes. It is true. It is. So. Yes. You are...absolutely right. You'll be
as immortal as the lobster you just ate.

DAUGHTER
I still don't feel anything.

FATHER
Maybe if you...keep eating.

The DAUGHTER continues to pick at and eat the lobster.

DAUGHTER
What was the bribe for?

FATHER
This was not a bribe.

DAUGHTER
Am I a disappointment?

FATHER
What? No! How could you-why would you-say that?

DAUGHTER
I heard mom telling Aunt Jay.

FATHER
That...?

DAUGHTER
You preferred boys.

FATHER
[...]

DAUGHTER
Is that true?

FATHER
That's not

DAUGHTER
Is it...?

FATHER
What she meant.//It's not what she meant.

DAUGHTER
What did she mean then?

FATHER
She meant that. I'm attracted to men. And not...women.

DAUGHTER
And mom is a woman.

FATHER
She is. Yes.

DAUGHTER
And you're not attracted to her anymore.

FATHER
It's not that simple.

DAUGHTER
And that's why she hates you?

FATHER
I can't speak for your mother.

DAUGHTER
She told Aunt Jay that she hated you.

FATHER
I wish she didn't say that but

DAUGHTER
Because you ruined her life.

FATHER
She might feel that way right now.

DAUGHTER
Am I gonna have two dads?

FATHER
Your mother's a beautiful woman and she's very young…

DAUGHTER
Jimmy O'Brien has two dads.

FATHER
Yeah?

DAUGHTER
Yup.

FATHER
He's a boy from your class?

DAUGHTER
Yup.

FATHER
And? Everybody knows? About…?

DAUGHTER
It's the 21st Century, dad.

FATHER
Yeah.

DAUGHTER
Everybody knows everything.

FATHER
As they should. I suppose. And? How do they. Everyone. Your classmates. Treat...Jimmy?

DAUGHTER
They treat him fine. Why?

FATHER
I mean, is everyone nice to him? Do people...like him?

DAUGHTER
Dad. He's the most popular kid in class.

FATHER
Yeah? That's...great.

DAUGHTER
Why wouldn't he be?

FATHER
No reason.

DAUGHTER
Mommy's Italian, right?

FATHER
You are all over the place.

DAUGHTER
And you're Irish?

FATHER
Only the good parts. That's what my grandmother would say.

DAUGHTER
And that makes me Italian and Irish, right?

FATHER
And then some.

DAUGHTER
But not French.

FATHER
Correct.

DAUGHTER
Jimmy O'Brien is French.

FATHER
Jimmy O'Brien is French?

DAUGHTER
You are so weird. Yes. That's what I just said.

FATHER
Ok. Maybe his…other dad…is…

DAUGHTER
Are you starting a new family?

FATHER
No. But I will have…someone…new…in my life. And when
you're ready, I'd love for you to meet him.

DAUGHTER
Is he French?

FATHER
Who?

DAUGHTER
Your new someone.

FATHER
His name is David.

DAUGHTER
That's a nicer name than what mommy called him.

FATHER
Oh. What did...? Nevermind.

DAUGHTER
Because if he were French, then maybe I could be French and
if I were French, I would get to work on the French project in
small groups with Jimmy O'Brien.

FATHER
How small are the groups?

DAUGHTER
So. Weird.

FATHER
I mean...would it be just you and Jimmy?

DAUGHTER
Mind you own business please.

FATHER
You're growing up so fast. I can't keep up.

DAUGHTER
Get over it.

FATHER
I will. Have to do that. But! It doesn't matter any way because
David is not French and even if he was, that wouldn't make
you French...necessarily...but maybe Jimmy O'Brien could
switch into your group because it sounds like Jimmy O'Brien
may have a little touch of the leprechaun in him.

DAUGHTER
Dad. Please. You're embarrassing me.

FATHER
Sorry.

DAUGHTER
Why did you stop loving mom?

FATHER
I didn't. Stop. Loving your mother.

DAUGHTER
Did you ever love her?

FATHER
Yes! Yes. Yes. I did and I still do. And someday you'll
understand

DAUGHTER
Did you ever love me?

FATHER
Sweetheart! Don't ever think that. Of course I love you. And I
will never, ever, stop loving you. Look at me: You are and
always will be the greatest thing that ever happened to me.
The single greatest thing. In my entire life.

DAUGHTER
Then why are you leaving us? If I'm the greatest thing that
ever happened to you, why are you leaving?

FATHER
I am not leaving you. And I know that might sound weird
because I'll be living in another home but

DAUGHTER
It's not fair.

FATHER
You're absolutely right: it's not. It's not fair to anyone. But
what I learned was: I have to be fair to me before I
could ever be fair to you or to mommy or to anyone.

DAUGHTER
What if I hate you?

FATHER
I really hope you won't. But I'd understand if you do. For now.

DAUGHTER
We'll just have to wait and see.

FATHER
I can accept that.

DAUGHTER
One more thing:

FATHER
Of course.

DAUGHTER
Can I have a lobster? You know. To bring home?

FATHER
You haven't finished this one. But we can box it. If you want. I
can//

DAUGHTER
I mean a live one. Like. As a pet.

FATHER
I don't think it works like that.

DAUGHTER
Mommy said you'd be in a very vulnerable state and I should
ask for something big.

FATHER
Mommy said a lot.

DAUGHTER
And that's what I want. That's the really big thing I want. One
of those really big lobsters. Because they made it this far and
they have the best chance. To never die. You know? And if
they never die, then they will never leave.

*The DAUGHTER works to remain strong but she cannot contain
the tears. In an instant, they stream down her face. The
FATHER is visibly affected and fights hard not to join her in
crying. He crosses to his DAUGHTER, takes her hands or her
face or her knees and kisses her as he says:*

FATHER
Hey. Hey. Hey. It's okay. You're allowed to cry. Go on. They're
a gift. Trust me on that. I am so, so sorry. I would never want
to hurt you. But I'm still learning about me just like you're
learning about you. This will be different for all of us. And it
will be hard. I know that. And I wish it didn't have to be. But I
promise you: this is how we'll grow. Ok? All of us. You get to
be your best you. And I'm gonna be my best me too. And, if
we keep an eye on each other...even if we live in different
houses...we will always be close. Trust me: We've made it this
far. Ok? And we're built to survive too. Don't you forget that.
Because that's exactly what we're gonna do.

The FATHER buckles.

FATHER
And I promise...I will never leave you.

The DAUGHTER pulls out of her tears for a moment.

DAUGHTER
Promise?

FATHER
Promise.

DAUGHTER
Is that a yes to the lobster?

The FATHER buckles again and clutches his DAUGHTER as the lights fade to black.

END OF PLAY

Unless, One Day, They Don't

By Emily Golden

About the playwright:

Emily Golden (she/her) is thrilled to have her play included in Hindsight 2023! A Seattle native, she holds an MFA in Creative Writing and Environment from Iowa State University where she currently teaches. Her play, Bethany Sees the Stars, premiered this past September at Copious Love in Seattle. Her short play, The Best We Can Do, also recently came in second in the festival of shorts at Edmonds Driftwood Players, and was featured as part of Fusion's Second Seven Readings in New Mexico, as well as by The Orange Players in Connecticut.

Emily is a proud member of the Dramatists Guild.

———————————————

UNLESS, ONE DAY, THEY DON'T was directed by Caitlin Strom-Martin.

SHANA	Lexus Fletcher
KENDRA	Caitlin Strom-Martin

CHARACTERS

SHANA
KENDRA

<u>Setting:</u> *Shana sits on a chair on one side of the stage. Kendra sits on a chair on the other side of the stage. Both face the audience. Neither is aware of the other.*

SHANA
Every day I watch from the window for my son to get off the school bus.

KENDRA
Every day I watch from the window to see my son rounding the corner from school.

SHANA
He's ten.

KENDRA
He's 13.

SHANA
Every day I watch from the window to see my son pull up in his car.

KENDRA
To see my daughter get dropped off.

SHANA
He's 17.

KENDRA
She's 16.

SHANA
Usually I'm folding laundry-

121

KENDRA
On a work call-

SHANA
Or starting dinner-

KENDRA
Work from home life.

SHANA
Sometimes I feel like I'm the last stay at home mom in the
world.

KENDRA
Some days I would kill to be a stay at home mom. Working
from home is the worst. I can see the mess but I still don't
have time to clean it up.

SHANA
I miss having my own life.

KENDRA
I miss my commute.

SHANA
My son's father picks him up because I don't get home from
work until 6.

KENDRA
My daughter stays at an after school program.

SHANA
I pick my daughter up from school every day. She's eight. She's
always smiling.

KENDRA
My son learned to roll his eyes two years ago and hasn't
stopped since.

SHANA
It's such a fun age.

KENDRA
When's the next fun age? 30? All I want is for him to get good enough grades to go to college. I think some space will do us good. Absence and fonder hearts and all that.

SHANA
She went to her first sleepover last summer. She had a blast. I cried myself to sleep. My husband reminded me that it was just one night. She'd be home in the morning.

KENDRA
My wife told me that she went through the same phase and I shouldn't worry. But I've seen her with her own parents and I don't think that was as much of a comfort as she thought it would be. If it's a phase, my wife has yet to grow out of it.

SHANA
When she's away from me I can still feel a thread connecting us. It stretches and stretches but never breaks.

KENDRA
I love him more than I can say.

SHANA
I love her more than I can say.

KENDRA
But some days I just want to strangle him.

SHANA
I watch at the window for my son to come home.

KENDRA
I watch at the window.

SHANA
And if he's late, I wait.

KENDRA
I wait.

SHANA
I wait.

KENDRA
I worry.

SHANA
I worry.

KENDRA
I try not to worry.

SHANA
The odds of something happening are...

KENDRA
Astronomical.

SHANA
Sure. It could happen.

KENDRA
But not to me.

SHANA
Not to my child.

KENDRA
My little girl.

SHANA
My little girl.

KENDRA
My little boy.

SHANA
My baby.

KENDRA
My kid.

SHANA
That happens to other people.

KENDRA
People on the news.

SHANA
In horrifying videos I can't help but watch.

KENDRA
He'll come home. I just have to be patient.

SHANA
She'll get home. There was traffic.

KENDRA
He stopped for gas.

SHANA
He missed his bus.

KENDRA
There are plans in place. There are protocols. Safety
measures. They have drills.

SHANA
She tells me the story of her cowering in the dark closet with
her classmates. They have to be quiet but it's hard because
most of them are crying.

KENDRA

He told me one of his teachers keeps a baseball bat in his room. Just in case.

SHANA

He says that they were told to ambush a shooter if he manage to get through the door. Throw things at him. Catch him by surprise.

KENDRA

His teacher will attack the shooter with the baseball bat. Put himself between the gun and the kids. I'm not sure a seventh grade science teacher should have to sign up for that.

SHANA

One of the other moms got her kid a bulletproof backpack. But they keep their backpacks in their cubbies out in the hall. Even if I got it for her, she wouldn't be able to get to it during a lockdown.

KENDRA

One of the teachers has a bucket and kitty litter stored in the classroom. In case any of the kids have to use the bathroom while they're locked down. Who thinks of these things?

SHANA

I hate that we have to think of these things.

KENDRA

They aren't allowed to carry backpacks or puffy coats through the halls.

SHANA

There are metal detectors at the entrance.

KENDRA

There's a police officer assigned to the school. They call him a "resource officer." He carries a gun.

SHANA

The resource officer arrested a twelve year old for yelling at a teacher last week. My kid says they didn't see it, but it was on the news.

KENDRA

My baby's scared of the resource officer. They don't like that there's a gun in school.

SHANA

Who trains the police officers? Who trains the teachers? I can't help but feel like anyone with a gun is just one more person who could potentially snap.

KENDRA

Am I supposed to trust these people? It's all well and good to give the good guys guns, but how are we sure who the good guys are?

.

SHANA

What if some kid steals a gun from one of the good guys? Parents are supposed to lock them up in a safe so kids don't accidentally get them. Statistically, just having a gun around raises your chances of being shot.

KENDRA

I took my daughter to talk to a therapist after their last lockdown drill. Nobody was warned about it in advance. The vice principle went through the halls pretending to be a shooter. Kids were calling their parents to say goodbye. My daughter said she didn't call me because she couldn't stop crying and she didn't want the last thing she said to me to sound scared. She wanted me to remember her happy.

SHANA

My kid was in the bathroom once during a lockdown drill. They have to use the bathroom in the nurse's office because the school won't let them use their preferred bathroom. They said the nurse climbed out the window and ran and just left them there. They asked me why the nurse didn't take them with her. I told them that sometimes when we're that scared our minds don't work right. We can't make real decisions, we just act.

KENDRA
The therapist said she had some PTSD symptoms from the lockdown drill. So now my daughter's traumatized by the way her school tried to prepare her for the potential of trauma. Who is that helping?

SHANA
Part of me wishes they would stop with the drills.

KENDRA
Part of me wants to homeschool.

SHANA
I wish I could homeschool.

KENDRA
I hate dropping him off.

SHANA
I don't like walking her to the bus stop in the morning.

KENDRA
I used to love having a few hours with the house to myself.

SHANA
I used to like the alone time.

KENDRA
Now I want to lock him up and not let him out of my sight.

SHANA

Every time I see a story about another school and they flash the pictures of the kids, it just makes me wonder—

KENDRA

How are we all still doing this?

SHANA

How are we just sending them to school like nothing's happening?

KENDRA

How many kids get on buses or bikes or climb out of their parents' cars and wave goodbye in their light up sneakers-

SHANA

Wearing Pokemon t-shirts-

KENDRA

With their new haircuts-

SHANA

Their lunchables-

KENDRA

Their fruit by the foot-

SHANA

Their texts from the girl they like but haven't had the guts to respond to-

KENDRA

And how many of them don't make it back?

SHANA

And mothers and fathers and siblings and friends think back on their last conversation and realize they have to be kind to everyone, every day, because last conversations don't

look any different than any other.

KENDRA

I tell her I love her every single morning as she gets out of the car even though it embarrasses her. Because I need to know that those were my last words to her.

SHANA

We fought the other morning. He wanted to wear ripped jeans to school and I wouldn't let him. I wouldn't let him leave until we made up. I started crying. He looked at me like I was crazy but he finally gave me a hug. He missed first period so I had to write him a note. He's really a great kid.

KENDRA

And then, once she's gone, I start the countdown.

SHANA

Seven hours until he's home.

KENDRA

Six hours until I have to leave to go pick her up.

SHANA

Until the minute when I see her out the window.

KENDRA

Until his bus pulls up and he comes out looking happy or tired or with gum in his hair or telling me he needs to make a diorama of the lifecycle of a jellyfish by tomorrow.

SHANA

She always wants a snack right away.

KENDRA

He gets to relax on his phone for half an hour before I make him start his homework.

SHANA
Most of the time I'm just chauffeuring him from school to soccer practice. I pack him a dinner to eat on the way.

KENDRA
She usually gets home before me but I make her text me as soon as she walks through the door so I know she's home safe.

SHANA
I breathe a sigh of relief.

KENDRA
I watch the news.

SHANA
I wonder about odds and statistics and how long this is going to go on if nothing changes.

KENDRA
If nothing changes, how can anything change?

SHANA
We know the outcome. If it goes on like this, we know how that ends.

KENDRA
And we wake up and do it all over.

SHANA
We watch out the window.
KENDRA
We welcome them home.

SHANA
We send them off to college.

KENDRA
We help them move into apartments.

SHANA
They go to malls and concerts and clubs and movie theaters
and grocery stores.

KENDRA
And we never relax.

SHANA
Not completely.

KENDRA
Until they come home.

SHANA
Unless.

KENDRA
One day.

SHANA
They don't.

END OF PLAY

The Equality Bureau

By Jada Thompson-McGuire

About the playwright:

Jada is a novice playwright and formerly failed poet, who grew up in upper-state New York. In 1997, she embarked on a year-long global journey, collecting exotic source material for her stories, and landed in the paradise of Sonoma County, where she mothers, writes, and helps make wine.

THE EQUALITY BUREAU was directed by Lennie Dean.

ALICE	Lexus Fletcher
Ms. TABER	Julianne Bradbury
Mr JENSEN	Ryan Severt

CHARACTERS

ALICE MATTHEWS-LEE: 42 years old, African-American, business professional, a citizen with a serious complaint.
MS. TABER: 60 years old, white, a Service Representative at the Equality Bureau.
MR. JENSEN: 25 years old, white male; Intake Counselor at the Equality Bureau.

Setting: Year 2030; mid-morning. Government office in Sacramento, CA.

// indicates an interruption. The next character's line begins at this point.

MS. TABER and MR. JENSEN sit working at service windows in a plain business office, like what you would find at a Department of Motor Vehicles. The line to the service windows is marked by guidance rope. The path is long and serpentine; no one is waiting. ALICE enters through a door, dressed in an attractive, professional outfit. Rather than trudge needlessly through the empty line, she walks directly to the front and waits to be called. MS. TABER and MR. JENSEN continue working at their monitors, not acknowledging ALICE's presence.

ALICE
Excuse me.

MS. TABER
Oh, hello.

MR. JENSEN
I didn't see you there.

MS. TABER
(*to MR. JENSEN*) Undoubtedly because she skipped the line.

ALICE
There was no one waiting.

MS. TABER
It doesn't matter.

ALICE
I would end up at the same spot either way, right?

MS. TABER
Not exactly. As you noticed, we did not see you waiting.

MR. JENSEN
We certainly would have noticed you waiting if you had
followed the prescribed pathway.

ALICE
I see. I will remember that for my next visit.

MS. TABER
Unfortunately, that will not do. We are obligated to treat
everyone equally and if we fail to do that, there will be
consequences for you and us.

MR. JENSEN
I would be most appreciative if you would return to the end of
the line and when you once again arrive at the front,
we will be happy to assist you.

ALICE
You're kidding.

*MS. TABER and MR. JENSEN return to their work and ignore
ALICE. ALICE returns to the rear, dutifully walks through the
path until she reaches the front, and waits at the designated
spot.*

MR. JENSEN
Good morning, how may I help you?

ALICE
I have come to complain about the equality certification
policy.

MR. JENSEN
Oh, that is not within my scope of responsibility. I handle
intake and assessments. Ms. Taber, right there, will be happy
to help you.

ALICE
So I have to go back to the end of the line?

MR. JENSEN
Don't be silly! We would never ask you to do that. Step right
over there and Ms. Taber will call you.

ALICE steps over to a waiting spot in front of MS.TABER.

MS. TABER
(Loudly.)
Next!

ALICE
Yes, I would like to file a complaint regarding the equality
certification policy.

MS. TABER
I see. What is your first name?

ALICE
Alice.

MS. TABER
Is that with one "A" or two?

ALICE
Who begins Alice with two "A"s"?

MR. JENSEN
Oh, you would be amazed at the variations, and we are
committed to respecting every citizen's preferred spelling.

ALICE
Have you ever met an Alice with two "A's"?

*MR. JENSEN and MS. TABER look at each other and shake
their heads no.*

MR. JENSEN
I assist people named Aaron, and that starts with two "A"s.
Therefore, any name starting with "A" could have repeating
"A"s.

ALICE
My name starts with one A...l-i-c-e.

MS. TABER
Last name?

ALICE
Matthews-Lee. M-A-T-T-H-E-W-S //

MS. TABER
That was two "T's" correct, not three?

ALICE
Yes, two "T"s. One hyphen, one "L", two "E"s.

MS. TABER
Not three, and not //

ALICE
Two "E"s.

MS. TABER
Very good. May I have your ECN please?

ALICE
What?

MS. TABER
Equality Certification Number.

ALICE
Oh, yes of course.

ALICE pulls out a card and hands it to Ms. Taber.

MS. TABER
You know, we now have a tattooist on site who can ink your rating and a scan-able ECN onto your arm, neck, or forehead. Then you don't need to bother with a card.

Ms. Taber reads aloud and types.

MS. TABER (CONT'D)
"S6A6T6AN". OK, let's see. What!? Mr. Jensen, I have an A+ here! That is an impressive equality rating Ms. Matthews-Lee. If we had known, we would have insisted that you skip the line entirely.

ALICE
That doesn't seem fair.

MR. JENSEN walks over to where MS. TABER is sitting, holding up his smart phone.

MR. JENSEN
I have never met an A+! I would be honored if you would take a selfie with me.

ALICE
I am sorry, I would rather not.

MR. JENSEN is surprised, then scowls. As he returns to his desk, he mutters.

MR. JENSEN
Oh, your high rating makes you too good for me.

MS. TABER
Well, we do this infrequently, but with an A+ rating, I am sure that we can arrange to meet you at your home in the future. After all, our mission is to assist the disadvantaged.

ALICE
No, I definitely do not want the Equality Bureau to visit my home.

MS. TABER
I see. Well, to address your inadequate rating, I am authorized, at my own discretion, to increment someone's rating by one level. In your case, I would be honored to immediately upgrade you to an exceedingly rare "A++"

MR. JENSEN again lifts up his smart phone.

MR. JENSEN
(*to Alice*) Please, a selfie?

ALICE
No. (*to MS. TABER*) Why do you assume that I am here because I am at any kind of disadvantage?

MS. TABER
Well, I would have to review your scoring sheet to learn the details, but right off the bat, you are a person of color, and...let me see...

139

MS. TABER searches her monitor screen.

MS. TABER (CONT'D)
...yes, you are a woman.

ALICE
I am, in fact, a privileged woman of color.

MS. TABER
No, you definitely are not. The ER is designed specifically to assign low ratings to privileged people. We are here to help underprivileged people such as yourself.

ALICE
I'm sure that you are a decent person and a hardworking bureaucrat, but I want you to understand that my high rating is a curse, not a blessing.

MS. TABER
That is simply impossible.

ALICE
Well, I am sharing with you from my lived experience.

MS. TABER
There must be a misunderstanding.

ALICE
I was raised in an affluent, educated, and emotionally supportive home.

MS. TABER
That's wonderful! See the equality rating system was effective for you.

ALICE
The Bureau didn't exist yet.

MS. TABER
We believe the Equality Bureau has improved society
retroactively.

ALICE
My husband has a rating of C, but he had far more obstacles in
his youth than I did. He immigrated from China when he was
10, learned English while being teased at school, and his single
mother worked 12 hours a day as a housekeeper. There is
something fundamentally unfair here.

MS. TABER
Actually, that sounds about right. Asians typically are rated
two grades below black people and one grade below brown
people.

ALICE
What!?

MS. TABER
(Suddenly nervous.) Hmm...I don't...I'm not...I misspoke. The
Bureau is supremely just and it knows who deserves
advantages and who does not.

MS. TABER types on her keyboard.

MS. TABER (CONT'D)
Let me take a look at your family record. Oh, I see that you
have a 20 year old daughter named Amari, and being a
mixedrace woman of color, she is rated "A". A double-A
household! Is she getting by OK?

ALICE
There is a serious problem. That is why I am here.

MS. TABER
Oh, no! We cannot tolerate a highly rated person being
mistreated. Please, how can I help?

ALICE
Amari is a second year student at M.I.T.

MS. TABER
What a lovely name! What does it mean?

ALICE
It means "fierce" in the Yoruba language. In Chinese it means
"immortal." And in Hebrew, "promised by God.

MS. TABER
Oh my, what an inspiring name! The Bureau certainly will do
everything in its power to nurture that aspiration. And
since she is studying at M.I.T., she represents another
success story for the Bureau.

ALICE
She is an extraordinary person, and in many ways she already
embodies her name...despite the Equality Bureau.

MS. TABER
Despite? You can't mean that.

ALICE
The Bureau is threatening to expel her from M.I.T.

MS. TABER
She must have done something terribly wrong, like offending
a professor or the Academic Equality Administrator.
Perhaps she committed a micro-aggression against a
student such as herself, a highly rated student prone to
crying.

ALICE
Amari does not cry easily, nor is she rude to professors,
administrators, and classmates. She only offended the Bureau.
After being at the university for 18 months--with a 4.0
GPA, I might add--the Bureau detected an irregularity

with her application. She entered a "C" for her equality rating, and "white" for her race.

MS. TABER
She lied! Of course the Bureau would be furious. Why would she do that?

ALICE
Because she is fierce and independent and wants to succeed on her own terms.

MS. TABER
Who does she think she is to decide the amount of help she needs? That is the Bureau's responsibility.

ALICE
Well it's doing a shitty job.

MS. TABER
I am detecting macro-aggressions from you Ms. Matthews-Lee! And after everything we have done for you people.

ALICE
"You people?"

MS. TABER
You know what I mean.

ALICE
Oh yes, I do know very much what you mean.

MS. TABER
The disadvantaged people we are helping.

ALICE
Like my daughter.

MS. TABER
We cannot let people break the rules or the entire system
will collapse.

ALICE
Precisely.

ALICE removes a clipboard from her purse.

ALICE (CONT'D)
I am circulating a petition to replace the Equality Bureau
with a program called the Poverty Reduction Initiative. My
team has collected 21,000 signatures in a mere two
weeks. Would you care to sign?

*MR. JENSEN moves covertly towards the entrance. Along the
way, he removes one of the guide ropes and carries it with
him.*

MS. TABER
And what can you possibly hope to achieve that the Bureau
hasn't already?

ALICE
Tangible, targeted, and continually improved investments in
impoverished communities. These are the people we know for
certain are underprivileged. They deserve superb education,
including pre-school, highquality healthcare, attractive
buildings, clean streets, and physical safety.

MS. TABER
The Bureau adamantly opposes increased funding for law
enforcement in poor, high-crime neighborhoods.

ALICE
I'm not surprised, because those communities in fact want
more policing and security.

MS. TABER

You know, Ms. Matthews-Lee, I've heard quite enough from you. We simply cannot let people like you undermine our beloved Equality Bureau.

MS. TABER makes a call on her desk phone.

MS. TABER (CONT'D)

Yes, I am invoking clause 34.1.7 of the 2027 Equality Act.

ALICE slowly backs away towards the entrance.

MS. TABER (CONT'D)

Please send two equalization officers to building six immediately. We have a double-red threat from a non-compliant A+. Yes, can you believe that, an A plus.

ALICE turns, walks towards the entrance, and discovers MR. JENSEN blocking the door.

MR. JENSEN

Ms. Taber!

MS. TABER looks up, still on the call. MR JENSEN prepares to bind ALICE with the rope.

MR. JENSEN (CONT'D)

Ask them to send the tattooist!

Lights dim to black.

END OF PLAY

A Nice, Quiet Neighborhood

By Ellen Sullivan

About the playwright:

Ellen Davis Sullivan is an award-winning writer of fiction, nonfiction and plays. Her one-act plays have been on stage in festivals across the country including The Boston Theatre Marathon, Indie Boots in Chicago and The Thalia Festival in New York City and have been published in Ponder Review and anthologies including The Best Ten-Minute Plays 2016 (Smith & Kraus). Ellen's essay, The Perfect Height for Kissing won the Columbia University Nonfiction Prize and appeared in Issue 53 of Columbia: A Journal of Literature and Art. Her stories have been published in print journals including Cherry Tree, Stonecoast Review and Moment Magazine and are online at OPEN: Journal of Arts and Letters and Cotton Xenomorph among others. Ellen is a member of the Dramatists' Guild.

A NICE, QUIET NEIGHBORHOOD was directed by Sky Hernandez-Simard.

LONG TIME RESIDENT	Peter Downey
KYLE	Sam Minnifield

CHARACTERS

LONG TIME RESIDENT: Soccer fan, White, who feels the world has changed in too many ways that aren't good. Age: 60-90, any gender.
KYLE: Soccer fan, BIPOC, who feels the world hasn't changed nearly enough. Age: 20-50, any gender.

Setting: The Present. A residential street.

KYLE enters with a vuvuzela. He blows on it, not a blast, just loud enough to produce an annoying buzz. Dances as if leading a parade.

KYLE

Who knows what democracy looks like? This is what democracy looks like.

LONG TIME RESIDENT

Hey! You with the noisemaker.

KYLE mimes innocence, Who me?

LONG TIME RESIDENT (CONT'D)

You see anyone else around here disturbing the peace?

KYLE

I'm not disturbing the peace. I'm standing up for what matters.

LONG TIME RESIDENT

Christ. One of them.

KYLE

Who's that?

LONG TIME RESIDENT

The only Black Lives Matter people.

KYLE
It's not only.

LONG TIME RESIDENT
But that's what you really mean.

KYLE
No. I don't.

LONG TIME RESIDENT
(Thinks for a second) So you're Antifa?

KYLE
There is no such thing.

LONG TIME RESIDENT
Course there is. I hear about it all the time.

KYLE
I hear about Martians. Doesn't mean they exist.

LONG TIME RESIDENT
I mean on the news.

KYLE
Let's not go there.

LONG TIME RESIDENT
So you won't admit you're one of them.

KYLE
I am not a Martian. *(Blows a short bleat on the vuvuzela)*

LONG TIME RESIDENT
Hey, you're busting my ear drums with that thing.

KYLE
(Looks at the vuvuzela) I don't think that's possible.

LONG TIME RESIDENT
So, you'd do it if you could?

KYLE
That's not why I'm here.

LONG TIME RESIDENT
Why are you here in our nice, quiet neighborhood?

KYLE
I know what that means.

LONG TIME RESIDENT
It means it was quiet until you showed up with your za-vu-
zela.

KYLE
Vuvuzela.

LONG TIME RESIDENT
I thought the World Cup banned those things.

KYLE
They did. So I'm stuck with it.

LONG TIME RESIDENT
You watch football?

KYLE
Most folks around here call it soccer.

LONG TIME RESIDENT
Now you're putting us in a box.

KYLE
All you quiet folks don't have much use for one of these.

LONG TIME RESIDENT
What're you driving at?

KYLE
Last night. You called the cops.

LONG TIME RESIDENT
We've got a noise ordinance. It won't stay a nice, quiet
neighborhood unless the rules are enforced.

KYLE
You've got a rule against girls giggling?

LONG TIME RESIDENT
They were doing a lot more than that. They were singing - and
dancing - right down the middle of the street.

KYLE
So you hear a couple teenagers singing and you call the
police?

LONG TIME RESIDENT
How d'you know it was me?

KYLE
That's why I brought this. *(Indicates the vuvuzela)* I figure
whoever called the cops on those girls would be out at the
first blast of this baby. *(Blows another short bleat on the
vuvuzela.)* No justice, no / peace.

LONG TIME RESIDENT
Stop that.

KYLE
I'm on a public street.

LONG TIME RESIDENT
You got a parade permit?

150

KYLE
(Turns around as if looking for followers) You see a parade?

LONG TIME RESIDENT
Wise ass.

KYLE
(Blows on vuvuzela) No justice, no peace. / No justice, no peace.

LONG TIME RESIDENT holds up their hands as if conceding the point. KYLE goes silent.

LONG TIME RESIDENT
Tell me one thing. You related to those girls?

KYLE
Brilliant deduction, Sherlock.

LONG TIME RESIDENT
I should've known you were from the same family. None of you have any respect for my ears - or the law.

KYLE
A noise ordinance isn't a law.

LONG TIME RESIDENT
So there are rules you follow and rules you break?

KYLE
(Examines car parked in driveway) I see you got a handicapped parking sticker.
LONG TIME RESIDENT
What about it?

KYLE
You got yourself out your front door pretty damn quick.

LONG TIME RESIDENT
My doctor says I don't pick up my feet high enough. I could trip and fall on uneven pavement.

KYLE
That the doc's idea or yours?

LONG TIME RESIDENT
I'm old. I'm entitled.

KYLE
You got that right.

LONG TIME RESIDENT
Anyway, it's been...I wouldn't say exactly nice chatting / with you—

KYLE
Know why it couldn't be nice?

LONG TIME RESIDENT
'Cause you keep blasting that horn?

KYLE
Because there's nothing nice about getting a young girl arrested for having a little fun.

LONG TIME RESIDENT
I didn't tell them to arrest anyone.

KYLE
It never occurred to you that's what would happen when you called the police?

LONG TIME RESIDENT
Cops give a lot of people warnings. Tell them to pipe down. Don't do it again.

KYLE
That's your experience of cops. Not mine.

LONG TIME RESIDENT
They must've been doing something for the cops to arrest
them.

KYLE
The cops saw what they look like and they're pretty sure they
don't belong on this nice, quiet street. That can be all it takes.

LONG TIME RESIDENT
I didn't know. I went into my house as soon as the police
showed up. I don't want any trouble. I turned down my
hearing aids and went to sleep.

KYLE
Maybe having 'em turned up is why you find normal sounds so
annoying.

LONG TIME RESIDENT
Those girls were singing loud as they could. That's not normal.

KYLE
You don't like singing?

LONG TIME RESIDENT
There's a time and place for it.

KYLE
Church choir?

LONG TIME RESIDENT
Definitely.

KYLE
Start of a Liverpool match?

LONG TIME RESIDENT
You root Liverpool? Figures.

KYLE
So you're Man U.

LONG TIME RESIDENT
United forever!

KYLE
Guess we're meant to be on opposite sides of everything.

LONG TIME RESIDENT
Not everything.

KYLE
How's that?

LONG TIME RESIDENT
That song you all sing. I kind of like it.

KYLE
You'll Never Walk Alone.

LONG TIME RESIDENT
I can never make out all the words what with them singing in
those accents of theirs.

KYLE
Did you turn up the old hearing aids?

LONG TIME RESIDENT
That's the trouble with these things. They make sound louder.
Not clearer.

KYLE
You can get the words to come up on your TV screen.

LONG TIME RESIDENT
That's what my granddaughter says. She told me what to do,
but I couldn't figure it out.

KYLE
I could show you.

KYLE moves toward RESIDENT's house.

LONG TIME RESIDENT
No need. I....

KYLE
Afraid I'll steal something.

LONG TIME RESIDENT
There's nothing in there worth taking. I just...it's not all neat
like it should be.

KYLE
You have a lot of ideas about how things should be. *(beat)* I
could teach you the words.

LONG TIME RESIDENT
Christ, no. I don't want to sing my enemy's fight song.

KYLE
We're opponents. We don't have to be enemies.

LONG TIME RESIDENT
Those Liverpool fans seem to think they're fighting an enemy
when they're singing.

KYLE
They're fighting to be themselves. You gotta stop thinking you
know everything about people from just knowing one thing.

LONG TIME RESIDENT
Those your words of wisdom?

KYLE
I do like the song says: Hold my head up high and walk with
hope in my heart.

LONG TIME RESIDENT
That's what they're saying?

KYLE
Yep.

LONG TIME RESIDENT
Well, I agree with that.

KYLE
Hold on. *(KYLE puts down the vuvuzela, takes out a cell phone,
looks up at the house, keys).* You'll be getting a poster with the
words. I picked one without the Liverpool seal.

LONG TIME RESIDENT
You didn't need to do that.

KYLE
No worries.

LONG TIME RESIDENT
Thank you. By the way, I won't be pressing charges or
anything.

KYLE
Thanks.

LONG TIME RESIDENT
Just 'cause you got me the words, don't expect me to be
singing the song.

KYLE

Never. But I'll sing it loud and clear. You'll probably hear me.
My house is just a couple streets over.

LONG TIME RESIDENT

You live in this neighborhood?

KYLE

Moved in during the winter. Had my first barbecue last night.
That's where my cousin was coming from.

LONG TIME RESIDENT

I haven't seen you before.

KYLE

Or heard me. I want to keep it a nice, quiet neighborhood.

LONG TIME RESIDENT

(Hesitates, then raises arm with closed fist) Welcome,
neighbor.

LONG TIME RESIDENT extends fist and they dap.

END OF PLAY

Credits

Playwrights

Michael P. Adams, Scott Carter Cooper, Emily Golden,

Allison Moon, Jessica Moss, Joni Ravenna, Dana Schwartz,

Ellen Sullivan, Jada Thompson-McGuire, Michael Towers,

Greg Vovos

Directors

Seth Dahlgren, Lennie Dean, Skylar Evans,

Sky Hernandez-Simard, Jenny Hollingworth, Cheryl King,

Caitlin Strom-Martin, Zane Walters, David L. Yen

Actors

Mark Anthony, Julianne Bradbury, Mark Bradbury,

Peter Downey, Lexus Fletcher, Anthony Martinez,

Sam Minnifield, Allie Nordby, Mike Pavone, Ryan Severt,

Caitlin Strom-Martin, Sylvia Whitbrook

The artists at Left Edge Theatre want to extend a huge thank-you to all the artists who participated in this festival and to the audience, who joined us.

Left Edge Theatre Staff

CHIEF ETERNAL OPTIMIST	Argo Thompson
ARTISTIC DIRECTOR	David L. Yen
HINDSIGHT 2023 FESTIVAL DIRECTOR	Jenny Hollingworth
CASTING DIRECTOR	Serena Elize Flores
TECHNICAL DIRECTOR	April George
SOUND DESIGNER	Joe Winkler
PRODUCTION MANAGER	Vicki Martinez
DEVELOPMENT COORDINATOR	Kimberly Kalember
BOX OFFICE MANAGER	Lulu Thompsxn
FRONT OF HOUSE MANAGER	Zane Walters
YOUTH PROGRAM DIRECTOR	Anthony Martinez
SOUND ENGINEER	Ryan Severt

———————————